AUSTRALIAN WINE

With Food

AUSTRALIAN WINE

With Food

MPC

Published by
Moorland Publishing Co. Ltd.
Moor Farm Road
Ashbourne, Derbyshire DE6 1HD

British Library Cataloguing in Publication Data
Cox, Jill
Australian Wine with Food
1. Australian Wines
I. Title
641.220994
ISBN 0-86190-401-X

From an original idea by Hazel Murphy of
the Australian Wine Bureau

Designed by **Casebourne Rose Design Associates**
Art Director: **Mike Rose**
Recipe development, food preparation for
photography and styling by
Diane Curtin and **Alison Grainge**
Photography by **Miki Moulton**
Illustration by **Sue Casebourne**
Culinary co-ordination by **Joyce Hardy**
Typesetting by **Parker Typesetting**
Hamper (p.58) courtesy of Asprey

Colour and black and white origination by
Scantrans, Singapore

Printed in Spain by **Graficas Reunidas, Madrid**

4

CONTENTS

INTRODUCTION

The Australian wine industry began some 200 years ago in Sydney, New South Wales. The first vines arrived with the original settlers in 1787 and were planted on the banks of the Parramatta in the city's suburbs – though few traces of these vineyards now remain.

The Hunter Valley region, internationally famous for its top quality wines, lies 160 kilometres to the north of Sydney. To the west is the Upper Hunter with its newer and more extensive vineyards.

In Victoria, the history of winemaking dates back to 1840. But it had a major setback due to an attack by the root attacking louse, Phylloxera, which all but destroyed the vineyards of Bordeaux in 1855. It happened in Victoria half a decade later and took many years for the problem to be overcome. To the centre of the State lies the Great Western, famous for its sparkling wine. This was where the goldrush happened – but the wines survived the gold.

The major wine-producing region is South Australia. Small garden plantings in Adelaide grew quickly into vineyards in the Adelaide Hills and north-east into the Barossa Valley. South Australia was colonised in 1836 and in 1837 vines from Tasmania were planted. Coonawara is an Australian name familiar to wine-drinkers all over the world. Vines have flourished in this rich patch of volcanic soil since the turn of the century, producing grapes generally accepted as the finest in Australia.

The first vineyards were planted in Australia shortly after the arrival of the first fleet in 1778

Western Australia has been making wine for more than 150 years. The Swan Valley, north of Perth, was the home of the first vines. But regions like Margaret River are demonstrating the exciting possibilities of Western Australian regions.

In fact, Australia is a wine-drinker's dream. Most of the major grape varieties are planted. Reds include Cabernet Sauvignon, Shiraz, Pinot Noir, Merlot and Malbec. The major whites are Sauvignon Blanc, Rhine Semillon, Chardonnay and Muscat.

The wines of Australia are now considered amongst the best in the world and there is something to suit every cuisine. But what to eat with Australian wines? There is no clearly defined national cuisine as there is with most of the other wine producing regions of the world. The truth of the matter is that there is an Australian wine to go with everything. There is no dish which is not well accompanied by a wine from Australia.

For an aperitif, a chilled sparkling wine or a crisp Sauvignon Blanc is a perfect choice. Chinese food is well-matched by a Rhine Riesling or Dry Muscat Blanc. Japanese? Choose a Chardonnay, Sauvignon Blanc or Sauvignon Blanc/Semillon.

Flavourful Italian food is perfect with a Shiraz, a Shiraz/Cabernet blend or Cabernet Sauvignon. And vegetarian dishes too mix well with just about any wine from Australia.

Red meats cry out for any Australian red wine. And even the most sophisticated fish dish is improved by a bottle of the country's Sauvignon Blanc, Sauvignon Blanc/Semillon, Semillon or Chardonnay.

But perhaps Australia's special and unique contribution to the wine drinking world is in the dessert department. A late-picked Muscat is a light wine which is grapey and aromatic with a delicate sweet flavour. Liqueur Muscats are fortified and have a heavy, liqueur style – the most delicious accompaniment to luscious puddings.

This book has been written to show that Australian wine is the best wine to drink with any food. Recipes from all over the world have been partnered by the wines of Australia – and these have proved to be the perfect choice in every case. Thirteen well-known wineries have a food section each and their wines have been matched with appropriate recipes in that section. For example, the wines of Penfold's have been chosen to accompany dishes in the chapter on barbecues, Rosemount wines are in the fish section and Tyrell's wines accompany Italian recipes.

However, any of the wines of each producer in the book could equally well suit a recipe from any of the other chapters as well as their own. Such is the versatility of the wines of Australia.

Berri Renmano

Berri Estates started life in 1916 making grape spirit from surplus dried sultanas, gordos and currants. A modest distillery was built in 1918. And in 1958 a separate winery was constructed which sold in bulk to other winemakers.

By 1970, wine was marketed under the Berri Estates label with the emphasis on quality and value for money.

The Renmano Grower's Distillery Ltd. was formed in 1914. Two years later, 130 local grape growers raised enough money to buy the winery as a going concern – the first co-operative winery in Australia. For the next 25 years the production was basically brandy, grape spirit and high quality dessert wines. As the winery grew in stature so did the winemaking facilities until it became one of the largest wineries in the Australian industry.

The result of a merger between two of Australia's largest and most respected wineries – Berri Estates and Renmano Wines – the new company, Consolidated Co-operative Wineries, is a major force in the Australian wine industry, making a substantial input to its development.

White Wines Berri Estates Semillon, Barossa Valley Sauvignon Blanc and Chardonnay
Red Wines Berri Estates Cabernet Sauvignon, Cabernet/Shiraz, Berri Barossa Valley Shiraz, Cabernet Sauvignon

Wolf Blass

Born in Germany in 1934, Wolf Blass was destined to be a winemaker. After school, he became an apprentice in viticulture and winemaking in the Lower Rhine and qualified after 3 years. He won his diploma in winemaking in Wurzburg, then trained in Reims studying Champagne-making. He moved to Australia in 1960 to work for Kaiser Stuhl Wines. After three years he became Australia's first freelance winemaker and by 1966 had produced red wine under the Blass name whilst still working for others.

In 1973 Wolf Blass Wines was founded and the company has enjoyed phenomenal success ever since, thanks to Wolf's expertise as a master winemaker and marketer. His wines are exported throughout the Pacific, to the States, Canada and the UK.

In 1984 the company went public, which made Wolf a millionaire overnight. Quelltaler Vineyards was bought by Wolf Blass Wines Ltd in 1987 and over $8 million has been spent transforming it into one of South Australia's premium wineries.

Red Wines Wolf Blass Black Label, President's Selection and Yellow Label
White Wines Wolf Blass Chardonnay and Rhine Riesling

The Wine Producing Regions of Australia

Australia is a vast continent (25 times larger than Britain) with a wide variation in climate and soils. The most northerly regions are too hot, arid, and tropical to sustain vineyards but grapes are grown extensively throughout the more southerly regions from east to west. This broad spectrum of microclimates enables Australia to produce wines diverse enough to match food from all over the world.

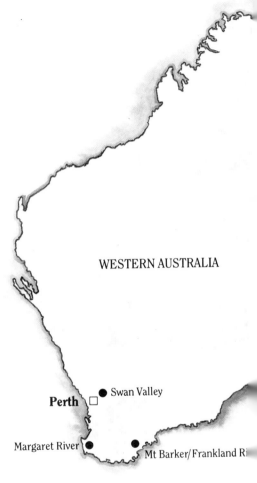

WESTERN AUSTRALIA

● Swan Valley

Perth □

Margaret River ●

● Mt Barker/Frankland Ri

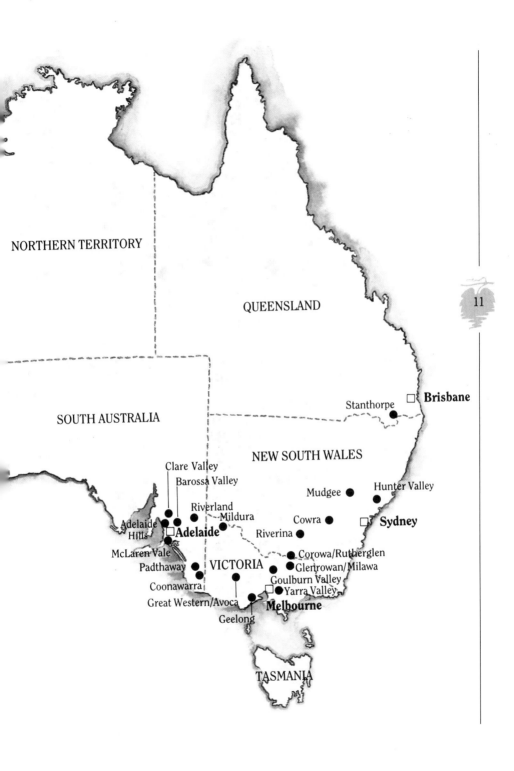

NORTHERN TERRITORY

QUEENSLAND

11

SOUTH AUSTRALIA

Stanthorpe ● □ **Brisbane**

NEW SOUTH WALES

Clare Valley
Barossa Valley

Mudgee ●   Hunter Valley ●

Riverland
Adelaide ●   Mildura ●
Hills   Cowra ●   □ **Sydney**
□ **Adelaide**   Riverina ●
McLaren Vale
Padthaway ●   VICTORIA ●   Corowa/Rutherglen
                        ● Glenrowan/Milawa
Coonawarra ●   Goulburn Valley
Great Western/Avoca ● □ Yarra Valley
                       ● **Melbourne**
Geelong ●

TASMANIA

Brown Brothers

John Francis Brown first planted grapes on the family property in 1885. His first vintage was in 1889, which was memorable not only because it marked the establishment of what is today one of the oldest family owned and operated vineyards in Australia, but also because it represented something of a break in tradition for the wine growing region in the north-east of Victoria. For many years this area had been famous for fortified wines, but John Francis Brown decided that the future of the vineyard lay in the production of table wines.

John Francis died in 1943 after his only son John Charles had taken over the business – still selling robust red wines and, in the 1960s, starting to bottle and sell whites. He now has four sons in the business.

With the wide spectrum of wines now produced, the company still respects the traditions of the area with its celebrated unique liqueur Muscats and Tokays.

White Wines Dry Muscat Blanc, King Valley Chardonnay, Semillon, Family Reserve Chardonnay
Red Wines Shiraz, Cabernet Sauvignon
Sweet Wines Late Picked Muscat, Orange Muscat & Flora, Noble Riesling

Hardy's

One of the great wine families of Australia, Hardy's has 4th and 5th generations in control of the company.

The business was started by a Devon farmer, Thomas Hardy, who arrived in Adelaide in 1850.

He worked for a year in John Reynell's vineyard but later left to go to the Victorian goldfields. When he returned to Adelaide, it was to marry his cousin Joanna. In 1853, he bought his first property on the banks of the Torrens which he called 'Bankside'. He made his first wine in 1857 and 2 years later began exporting wine back to England.

Within ten years he was making over 50,000 litres of wine from his own vineyards and also bought in grapes from other growers for his blends. In 1876, he bought the Tintara vineyard in McLaren Vale and expanded this by buying some adjoining land.

In 1887 he formed Thomas Hardy & Sons with his three sons. At the turn of the century, this became the largest wine producer in South Australia. Thomas died in 1912, just before his 82nd birthday.

Now his children and grandchildren control the company whose wines are among the best known in Australia.

In recent years the company has established an enviable reputation with its new wines such as the 'Hardy Collection' and the 'Bird Series' – some of the finest wines from Australia.

White Wines The Bird Series Chardonnay, Gewürztraminer/Riesling, The Hardy Collection Chardonnay, Semillon/Chardonnay, Nottage Hill Chardonnay
Red Wines The Bird Series Shiraz, Cabernet/ Shiraz, The Hardy Collection Cabernet Sauvignon, Nottage Hill Cabernet Sauvignon
Sparkling Wines Hardy's Grand Reserve, Grand Reserve Rosé

Lindemans & Rouge Homme

A young doctor from London, Henry John Lindeman emigrated to Australia in 1840 and became a general practitioner in the Lower Hunter Valley. Two years later he bought a farm and planted vines, but the vineyard was destroyed by fire in 1851. By 1860 he had rebuilt his winery and began bottling his wines in Sydney. He died in 1881 after handing control of the company over to his sons, Charles, Arthur and Herbert. Under their direction, Lindemans became one of the most successful wine exhibitors in the country. The expansion that followed included buying the re-named Pokolbin winery, the Coolalta vineyard, Warrawee and Sunshine amongst others. In 1965 the company acquired Rouge Homme, a rough translation of the name of the owners, a family called Redman, who established their vineyard in Coonawarra. Rouge Homme has one of Coonawarra's most sophisticated and modern wineries, and the wines produced on the estate can truly be called 'Coonawarra's finest'. Lindemans was one of the first Australian wine producers to win international recognition and awards for its wines in Bordeaux, London and Paris. The latest accolade was 'International Winemaker of the Year' awarded at the London International Wine and Spirit Competition.

White Wines Bin 95 Sauvignon Blanc, Bin 65 Chardonnay, Padthaway Sauvignon Blanc and Chardonnay
Red Wines Bin 50 Shiraz, Pyrus, St. George, Limestone Ridge

Mildara

The Canadian-born Chaffey brothers were responsible for the origins of Mildara Wines. Coming from a successful farming family in Ontario, the Chaffeys were well established in Canada when they were invited to look at Mildara on the Murray River.
They saw the potential for vines and in 1888 built a winery to make both table wines and brandy. What seemed at first to be a success gradually failed. A second venture was also disappointing – but a third attempt proved successful. This was Mildara Wines. In the ensuing year Mildara thrived and the company went from strength to strength.
Krondorf was one of the Mildara aquisitions which was already well-established as one of Australia's better middle-sized wineries, producing respected high quality wines.
Many know Mildara for brandies. But today their premium wines from Coonawarra, Eden Valley and Yellowglen have built up their now enviable reputation for excellence in table wines.

White Wines Mildara Flower Label Sauvignon Blanc, Church Hill Chardonnay, Jamieson's Run Coonawarra Chardonnay, Krondorf Semillon, South Australia Chardonnay
Red Wines Jamieson's Run, Mildara Coonawarra Shiraz, Mildara Cabernet Sauvignon, Cabernet Sauvignon/Merlot, Krondorf Shiraz/Cabernet

Mitchelton

Mitchelton is a unique kind of winery, curiously situated surrounded by an entertainment complex with swimming pools, restaurant, and picnic and barbecue areas.

First planted in 1969 on the banks of the Goulburn River, the winery was not an instant success. The river burst its banks and flooded the cellar, which was the first of a number of financial crises. The vineyard eventually changed hands.

By the late 1970s Mitchelton's reputation was well established as a maker of high quality wines.

The Valmorbida family now owns Mitchelton. They have a second vineyard in Styrathbogie Ranges and also buy in grapes to give an annual production which is among the largest in Victoria. Particularly noted for their Rhine Riesling, medals and accolades have rained on this company who, though still young, are recognised throughout Australia for wines that are consistent winners of gold medals.

White Wines Mitchelton Goulburn Valley Rhine Riesling, Marsanne, Reserve Chardonnay, Thomas Mitchell Fumé Blanc
Red Wines Mitchelton Goulburn Valley Cabernet Sauvignon, Thomas Mitchell Cabernet/Shiraz, Mitchelton CabMac

Orlando

Orlando was one of the first companies to become established in the Barossa Valley. In 1847, a young German, Johann Gramp, planted the first vines at Jacob's Creek in the Barossa Valley. Wine was made on a small scale for some years. But with time, the vineyards, cellars and winery were all enlarged to the extent that Orlando is one of the leading wine concerns in the Southern hemisphere.

The development was initiated mostly by Johann's son Gustav, born in 1850, and grew progressively under the guidance of his sons and later grandsons.

The company is now one of the three largest in the Australian wine industry. Throughout its history, Orlando has based its reputation on the consistent quality of its products. This dedication combined with up-to-date winemaking expertise has been rewarded by incredible success on the Australian Wine Show circuit. Orlando has become known throughout the industry as 'The Premium Quality Wine Company'.

White Wines Gramps Chardonnay, RF Chardonnay, RF Sauvignon Blanc, St. Hilary Chardonnay, Jacob's Creek Dry White and Medium Dry White
Sparkling Wines Carrington Extra Brut and Sparkling Rosé
Red Wines Gramps Cabernet/Merlot, RF Cabernet Sauvignon, Jacob's Creek Dry Red

14

Night harvesting in Australia

Penfolds

The Penfold-Kaiser-Stuhl-Seaview complex at Barossa Valley ranks among the world's largest wine production centres. It was founded in the mid 1800s – primarily for medicinal purposes but in the last 25 years has grown from a substantial family concern to Australia's biggest wine producer.

Penfolds' founder was Dr. Christopher Rawson Penfold, the immigrant son of a Sussex vicar. He arrived in 1844 and settled in Magill in Adelaide in a cottage he called The Grange. He planted a vineyard mostly as a natural cure for anaemia which he felt wine cured. His daughter Georgina married Thomas Hyland in 1861.

By 1885 Georgina and Thomas were making nearly half a million litres of wine a year. Their two sons Frank and Herbert eventually came into the business and between them they continued to expand. The Grange cottage built by Dr. Christopher Penfold is now a museum. But it gave its name to the wine which is probably Australia's most celebrated and certainly its most expensive: Penfolds Grange Hermitage.

Seaview vineyards dating from 1850 now belong to Penfolds. Its enormously successful Methode Champenoise sparkling wines are made in huge cellars in the Penfold complex.

White Wines Bin 202 Gewürztraminer/Riesling, Penfolds Semillon/Chardonnay and Chardonnay
Red Wines Dalwood Shiraz/Cabernet, Koonunga Hill Shiraz/Cabernet, Bin 128, Bin 28 Shiraz, Bin 389, St. Henri Cabernet/Shiraz
Sparkling Wines Seaview Chardonnay, Seaview Brut

Rosemount

In 1864 a German settler, Karl Brecht, planted vineyards in the Upper Hunter Valley. These produced such impressive wines that they were recognised with Gold medals in the Great Exhibitions of Europe and the USA. When Karl died, the vineyard reverted to pasture land.

In 1969, the property was purchased by the Oatley family who extensively replanted the vineyard, which took four years. In 1977 Bob Oatley bought Wybong Park winery and vineyard and several others followed. In 1983, he expanded further, acquiring the Mount Dangar vineyard, and in 1984 a large plot of land at Wybong Park, which is so far undeveloped.

Rosemount is still a family business and one of the best-known medium-sized wineries in Australia, particularly noted for its prestige quality wines. The success of Rosemount has been achieved by a successful marriage of traditional wine-making methods and modern technology.

White Wines Diamond Dry White, Rosemount Fumé Blanc, Chardonnay Wood Matured Semillon and Show Reserve Chardonnay, Giant's Creek Chardonnay, White's Creek Semillon, Roxburgh Chardonnay
Red Wines Rosemount Shiraz, Pinot Noir, Coonawarra Cabernet Sauvignon, Giant's Creek Pinot Noir, Kirri Billi Merlot, Kirri Billi Coonawarra Cabernet Sauvignon, Rosemount Dry Red, Kirri Billi Merlot

Seppelt

Seppelt Wines were founded by Joseph Seppelt who arrived in Australia from Silesia in 1849. Two years later he bought property in the Barossa Valley, now known as Seppeltsfield, and created what has become one of Australia's leading wine companies.

The first Seppelt wines were made in the family dairy but in 1867 Joseph Seppelt built his own winery. On his death the following year the winery was inherited by Joseph's son, Benno, then 21. It was his influence which earned Seppelt its reputation for quality wines.

By 1875 the cellar had doubled in size and continued to expand to a production figure of 1.8 million litres by the turn of the century. Benno's son, Oscar, took over after his fathers' retirement and continued the expansion programme. Seppelt is recognised throughout the world as a maker of premium quality wines. As Australia's most successful exhibitor with over 135 years of winemaking experience, Seppelt is firmly established as a leading winemaker with a range of award-winning wines.

White Wines Moyston Dry White, Moyston Medium Dry White, Gold Label Semillon/ Chardonnay and Chardonnay, Premium Chardonnay
Red Wines Moyston Red, Gold Label Shiraz/ Cabernet and Cabernet Sauvignon, Seppelt's Black Label Cabernet Sauvignon and Shiraz, Premier Vineyard Selection
Sparkling Wines Great Western Imperial Reserve and Brut Reserve, Great Western Rosé, Brut and Chardonnay

Tyrrell's

The Tyrrell family is one of the great names in the Australian wine industry. William Tyrrell came originally from Hampshire and became the first Bishop of Newcastle in Queensland. In 1850, three of his nephews moved to New South Wales. The youngest was Edward Tyrrell, at that time a teenager.

He tried dairy farming – a venture which was not successful. Next, he bought a plot of land in the Lower Hunter and started a vineyard. By 1870 Edward Tyrrell's property, named Ashmans, had 30 acres of vines established.

He married Susan Hungerford in 1873 and over the next decade or so produced 10 children, the eldest of which was Dan and the youngest Avery, who both eventually took over the running of the business.

Dan became the legendary winemaker who devoted his life to his trade. He had no children, but his brother did. It was Avery's son Murray who took over the company just before Dan died in 1959. Under Murray's guidance, the Tyrrell company flourished even further. His son Bruce is now in the family business and has two young sons of his own. So it seems there will be a fifth generation of Tyrrells ready to take over.

White Wines Hunter Valley Semillon/Sauvignon Blanc, Vat 47 Pinot Chardonnay, Long Flat White
Red Wines Hunter Valley Cabernet/Merlot, Cabernet Sauvignon and Pinot Noir, Long Flat Red

Wyndham Estate

Wyndham Estate is Australia's oldest operational winery and the Hunter Valley's largest and most successful wine group. The winery is situated on the banks of the Hunter River and is the headquarters of a group which has acquired major interests in the Hunter Valley.

The original winery was established by an English nobleman, George Wyndham, in 1828. A pioneer in every sense of the word, he built his own imaginative home, now being completely restored.

The winery quickly enjoyed remarkable growth and was gradually extended and passed on to the two sons, John and Alexander.

John died in 1887 and during the 1890s the winery passed out of Wyndham hands. For a spell it belonged to Penfold's and was later sold to Percy McGuigan, a Penfold's winemaker. It was his son Brian who headed a group of businessmen who founded Wyndham Estate, virtually re-instating the property to what it was a century before.

Wyndham has been extending its Hunter interests under Brian's leadership. The McGuigans have been the driving force behind the Wyndham Estate since the late 1960s. Brian's ability to make wines which find ready acceptance, together with his undoubted marketing and entrepreneurial skills, have ensured Wyndham's powerful presence on the Australian wine map.

White Wines Bin 222 Chardonnay, Bin TR2 Gewürztraminer/Riesling, Oak Cask Chardonnay, Verdelho, Hunter Chardonnay, Homestead Ridge Semillon/Chardonnay
Red Wines Bin 444 Cabernet Sauvignon, Bin 555 Shiraz, Bin 333 Pinot Noir, Homestead Ridge Shiraz/Cabernet
Sparkling Wines Semillon Cuvé Brut

A GREEK FEAST

The richly flavoured rustic cuisine of Greece is well matched by the excellent wines from Australia. Mildara Chardonnay, for example, has a fresh, lightly wooded style – excellent with white meats and salads. The famous Jamiesons Run Coonawarra Red is richly fruity and a perfect accompaniment to the slow-cooked Stifado – a stew of mixed meats in wine. And try Mildara's Cabernet Merlot with its soft fruitiness with roasts, grills and cheese dishes.

Drink the fragrant Mildara Murray River Valley Sauvignon Blanc with any seafood dish. Its intense fruitiness is a good complement.

Krondorf Semillon has a hint of vanilla on the bouquet with a crisp, dry and satisfying fruit character. Great with white meats, this is also a good match with delicately flavoured Lamb Meatballs with Oregano – but it makes a delicious aperitif served chilled, too.

But try the Krondorf Chardonnay with its big, full flavour and elegant fruit with well flavoured fish or chicken dishes with a sauce.

CLOCKWISE FROM TOP LEFT:
Greek Salad, Lamb Meatballs with Oregano, Mushrooms with White Wine and Mint

Greek Salad

*Colourful Mediterranean salad of fruity tomatoes
and olives in a lemony dressing*

SERVES 4
3 large beef tomatoes, washed
1 cucumber, washed
8 spring onions, trimmed
12 large black stoned olives
8oz/225g feta cheese, cubed

Dressing
6 tbsp fruity olive oil
2 tbsp lemon juice
salt and freshly ground black pepper
1 tbsp fresh coriander, chopped

Quarter tomatoes and cut cucumber into chunks. Place in a large serving bowl. Chop spring onions and add to bowl with olives. Sprinkle over feta.

Shake dressing ingredients together in a screw top jar and drizzle over the salad. Gently toss to coat. Serve immediately.

Mushrooms with White Wine and Mint

*Succulent button mushrooms marinated in
white wine with mint and shallots*

SERVES 4
1lb/450g button mushrooms
3 shallots, peeled and finely chopped
2 cloves garlic, crushed

For the marinade
¼pint/150ml olive oil
juice of 1 lemon
½ wineglass of white wine
pinch of sugar
2 tbsp fresh mint, shredded
salt and freshly ground black pepper
mint sprigs to decorate

Wipe mushrooms, trim stalks and place in a bowl with shallots and garlic. Mix marinade ingredients together and pour over mushrooms. Cover and leave for at least two hours, or even better overnight. Spoon mixture over occasionally to coat all the mushrooms.

Serve decorated with mint sprigs and with chunks of warm crusty bread.

Taramasalata with Red Lumpfish Roe

Smooth and velvety luxurious pale pink
dip speckled with red roe

SERVES 4

12oz/375g smoked cod's roe, skinned
1 onion, peeled and grated
1 clove garlic, peeled and crushed
3oz/75g fresh white breadcrumbs
grated zest and juice of 1 lemon
1/2 pint/300ml olive oil
freshly ground black pepper
2 tbsp red lumpfish roe
1/2 tbsp parsley, finely chopped

Purée cod's roe in a blender until smooth. Add onion, garlic, bread and lemon juice and mix in. Drizzle in olive oil in a thin stream, blending slowly until the mixture thickens. Spoon into a pot and season with pepper. Mix in lumpfish roe and parsley. Chill for an hour before serving.

Lamb Meatballs with Oregano

Lamb meatballs fragrantly flavoured with fresh oregano
and served with a delicate yogurt sauce

SERVES 4

1 1/2 lb/700g minced lamb
1 onion, peeled and grated
2 cloves garlic, crushed
squeeze of lemon juice
2 tsp fresh oregano, chopped
salt and freshly ground black pepper
beaten egg to bind

For the sauce
2oz/50g butter
1/2 tsp ground cumin
2 tbsp flour
1/2 pint/300ml milk
2 tbsp Greek yogurt
salt and freshly ground black pepper
grated cheese for sprinkling

Mix lamb, onion, garlic, lemon juice and oregano together and season with salt and pepper. Gradually add enough egg to bind and shape into even sized balls.

For the sauce, melt butter in a pan and add cumin. Cook gently for 1 minute. Add flour and stir in, then cook for an extra minute. Remove from heat and gradually add milk. Bring to the boil, stirring to thicken. Add yogurt and season with salt and pepper.

Fry meatballs in oil until browned, then place in an ovenproof dish. Pour over sauce and sprinkle with cheese. Bake in a preheated oven at Gas 6 400F 200C for 20 minutes or until cooked through.

Stifado

*Rich, robust pork and beef stew slowly
cooked in red wine with herbs*

SERVES 4

*2 tbsp olive oil
1 large onion, peeled and chopped
3 cloves garlic, crushed
1lb/450g pork, cut into cubes
1lb/450g stewing beef, trimmed and cut
into cubes
2 beef tomatoes, wiped and roughly
chopped
1 wineglass dry red wine
1/2 pint/300ml beef stock
salt and freshly ground black pepper
2 sprigs each, oregano, rosemary,
parsley tied together with 1 bay leaf*

Heat oil in a large pan and fry onion and garlic until soft, then remove from pan. Add pork and beef and fry until browned all over. Stir in tomatoes, wine and stock. Season with salt and pepper and add herbs. Bring to the boil, cover with a tightly fitting lid and simmer gently for 1½ hours or until meat is tender. The juices should have almost evaporated. 30 minutes before end of cooking time add onions and simmer until all is cooked. Discard herbs before serving.

Baklava

Sweet and sticky Greek pastries often served as a dessert – easy to make and absolutely delicious

SERVES 4
16 sheets of filo pastry
4oz/100g butter, melted
*4oz/100g blanched almonds, finely
    chopped*
1 tbsp caster sugar
6 tbsp runny honey
juice of ½ lemon

Lightly butter an oblong baking tin. Line with a sheet of filo trimmed to the same size as the tin. Brush with butter and top with another sheet of filo. Repeat layers until 8 sheets of pastry are used. Sprinkle over nuts and sugar and top with a further 8 sheets of filo, brushing well in between with butter. Cut into squares and bake in a preheated oven at Gas 4 350F 180C for 30 minutes or until golden and crisp.

Meanwhile warm honey with lemon juice. Remove baklava from the oven and pour over syrup. Leave to cool completely before serving in squares.

23

Yogurt and Brown Sugar

Smooth and sensuous yogurt cream layered with brown sugar which amazingly dissolves to give a marbled effect

SERVES 4
¾ pint/425ml plain yogurt
*¼ pint/150ml double cream, lightly
    whipped*
2 tbsp soft dark brown sugar

Mix yogurt and cream together. Spoon into serving glasses and sprinkle a little brown sugar over each. Chill overnight, to allow the sugar to marble through the yogurt cream.

SEPPELT
BEAUTIFUL BRUNCH

The perfect time for weekend entertaining which falls somewhere between breakfast and lunch – brunch. Get off to a good start with a glass of something sparkling – like the delicious Great Western Chardonnay, palest lemon coloured with green tints. The rich creamy flavour and crisp bubbles make this the perfect aperitif. What better to follow than an Australian Shiraz like Seppelt's Great Western Shiraz? Packed with spicy blackcurrant fruit, this matches an enticing platter of luxury fillet steak sandwiches. Salmon Kedgeree is a traditional English breakfast dish which works well for brunch too – especially accompanied by the Seppelt oak-matured Barooga Chardonnay with its full bodied and flavoursome, buttery taste. Rutherglen Show Muscat DP63 is the perfect liqueur to sip with a post-brunch Banana Brulée.

——Fillet Steak Sandwiches with Horseradish——

Delicious sandwiches with a macho filling

SERVES 4
8 slices white bread, toasted and lightly buttered
4 thin slices fillet steak
salt and freshly ground black pepper
2 tbsp oil
4 tbsp creamed horseradish sauce
1 lettuce heart, leaves separated and washed
4 tomatoes, sliced

Remove crusts from toast. Season steak with salt and pepper and flash fry in hot oil. Arrange on 4 slices of bread and top with horseradish. Place lettuce and tomatoes on top and finish with remaining toast. Cut into triangles and serve with points upwards.

Frilly Filo Pie

Layered potato pie in a crisp and frilly
filo pastry crust

SERVES 4–6
2lb/900g large potatoes, peeled
2 tbsp sunflower oil
1oz/25g butter
1 Spanish onion, peeled and thinly sliced
2 cloves garlic, crushed
few sprigs fresh thyme, chopped
salt and freshly ground black pepper
11oz/300g pack filo pastry
melted butter for brushing
3oz/75g Gruyère cheese, grated

Thinly slice potatoes and rinse well in cold water. Cook in lightly salted boiling water until only just tender. Drain and cool.

Heat oil and butter in a pan and gently fry onion and garlic with thyme until softened. Season with salt and pepper and leave to cool.

Lightly oil the base and sides of an 8"/20cm loose bottomed sandwich tin. Carefully line the base and sides with four sheets of filo pastry, brushing with melted butter between each layer. Place a layer of potatoes in the base, then a layer of onions, then a layer of cheese. Repeat layers, finishing with a layer of potatoes. Season well in between. Cover top with two sheets of filo and seal edges, brushing in between and on the top. Cut remaining filo into squares and brush with butter. Gently scrunch each square and arrange on top to make a frilly pattern. Bake in a preheated oven at Gas 4 350F 180C for 25 minutes. Cover top with foil if it becomes too brown. Serve hot or cold cut into wedges.

Goujons of Chicken

Tender strips of chicken deep-fried with a
crust of spicy breadcrumbs

SERVES 4
4 boneless chicken breasts, skinned
4 tbsp fresh white breadcrumbs
2 tsps Five Spice powder
salt and freshly ground black pepper
flour, sifted
2 eggs, beaten
oil for frying
spring onion brushes, for decoration

Cut chicken into thin strips. Mix breadcrumbs with Five Spice, salt and pepper. Dip chicken into flour and shake off excess. Dip in egg and then with breadcrumb mixture. Deep fry in hot oil until golden and cooked through. Serve decorated with spring onions.

CLOCKWISE FROM TOP LEFT:
Frilly Filo Pie, Red Salad, Smoked Salmon Kedgeree, Banana Brulée, Fillet Steak
Sandwiches

Baby Mille Feuilles

*Little puff pastry bites with
savoury fillings*

SERVES 4
8oz/225g ready made puff pastry
1 egg, beaten, to glaze
*sesame seeds, toasted, and black poppy
seeds to decorate*

For the fillings:

Anchovy butter
4oz/100g unsalted butter, softened
2 tbsp anchovy fillets, mashed
squeeze lemon juice
freshly ground black pepper

Herby cream cheese
4oz/100g cream cheese, softened
*2 tbsp mixed fresh basil, parsley and
chives, finely chopped*
salt and freshly ground black pepper

Roll out pastry on a lightly floured board
to ½"/1cm thickness. Cut small rounds
with a plain pastry cutter and place on a
buttered baking sheet. Chill for 30
minutes. Brush with egg, sprinkle half the
rounds with sesame seeds and remainder
with poppy seeds. Bake in a preheated
oven at Gas 6 400F 200C for 5 minutes or
until golden, well risen and crisp.

To make the anchovy butter, place all
ingredients in a bowl and mix well to
combine. Chill until ready for serving. For
the herby cream cheese, mix ingredients
together and season with salt and pepper.
Chill until needed.

Split the sesame topped rounds in half
horizontally. Spoon anchovy butter into a
piping bag and pipe swirls onto the bottom half of the rounds. Top with lids. Cut
remaining poppy seed topped rounds in
half and pipe swirls of herby cream cheese
on the bottoms. Top with lids. Arrange on
a platter and serve immediately.

Red Salad

*Mixture of different red salad vegetables for a
stunning crunchy salad*

SERVES 4
1 radicchio, trimmed and washed
8oz/225g cherry tomatoes, quartered
8oz/225g radishes, trimmed
1 red onion, peeled and sliced

For the dressing
6 tbsp sunflower oil
2 tbsp white wine vinegar
½ tsp mustard
salt and freshly ground black pepper

Seperate lettuce leaves and place in a
bowl. Add tomatoes, radishes and onions.

Shake all dressing ingredients in a screw
top jar. Drizzle over salad and gently toss
through to coat. Pile into a pretty bowl to
serve.

Smoked Salmon Kedgeree

Luxurious rice and fish dish which used to be an old-fashioned breakfast but is now frequently served as a buffet dish – especially for a brunch

SERVES 4

8oz/225g long grain rice
½ tsp turmeric
1oz/25g butter
1 small onion, peeled and finely chopped
4 slices smoked salmon, cut into strips
1 tbsp capers
salt and freshly ground black pepper
2 hardboiled eggs, shelled
½ tbsp finely chopped parsley

Cook rice in lightly salted boiling water with turmeric until tender. Drain. Melt butter in a pan and fry onion until softened. Stir in rice, salmon, capers and seasoning. Pile onto a warmed serving plate. Thinly slice eggs and cut slices into quarters to decorate kedgeree. Sprinkle with a little parsley.

Banana Brulée

Sensuous and creamy custard with bananas in the base, topped with crackly caramel

SERVES 4

2 bananas, peeled and sliced
lemon juice
1 pint/600ml double cream
1 vanilla pod
4 egg yolks
2 oz/50g caster sugar
2oz/50g icing sugar, sifted

Arrange banana slices in the base of 4 small ovenproof dishes. Pour cream into a bowl over a pan of simmering water. Add the vanilla pod. Beat egg yolks and caster sugar until light and creamy. Gradually pour over cream, stirring until blended. Pour mixture into dishes and stand them in a roasting tin. Pour in enough water to come halfway up their sides. Bake in a preheated oven at Gas 2 300F 150C for 1 hour or until the egg mixture has set. Remove, leave to cool completely and chill. Just before serving sprinkle a little icing sugar over each. Heat a metal kebab skewer over a flame and scorch criss cross patterns over to decorate.

The Dinner Party

One of the great successes of the Australian wine industry, the wines of Wolf Blass well match a sophisticated dinner party. Gold Label Riesling with its crisp fruitiness, for example, is the perfect aperitif served with Crab Tartlets. Wolf's own Caesar Salad is well complemented by his grassy, buttery South Australian Chardonnay. The Duck with Cherries calls for his Yellow Label Cabernet Sauvignon with its oaky blackcurrant aroma and sturdy flavour. Or choose the President's Selection Black Label with its soft, round fruit.

TOP TO BOTTOM:
Wild Mushroom Stew with Garlic and Pinenuts, Noodles with Chive Butter, Duck with Cherries

Crab Tartlets with Egg and Lemon

Tiny appetisers to serve with the
pre-dinner aperitif

SERVES 4
8oz/225g shortcrust pastry

For the filling
8oz/225g fresh crabmeat
juice of ½ lemon
salt and freshly ground black pepper
2 eggs, hardboiled and finely chopped

Roll out pastry on a lightly floured board to a thickness of ¼"/0.5cm. Lightly grease a tartlet tin and cut out rounds slightly bigger than the individual moulds using a fluted round pastry cutter. Gently ease circles into moulds and chill for 30 minutes. Bake blind in a preheated oven at Gas 6 400F 200C until just crisp and golden. Leave to cool slightly then carefully lift off onto a wire rack to cool completely.

For the filling, flake crabmeat into a bowl and remove any shell or bones. Mix with lemon juice and seasoning and spoon a little into each pastry case. Sprinkle with chopped egg to serve.

Noodles with Chive Butter

Herby pasta, served twirled into plaits,
is a good accompaniment to the duck

SERVES 4
12oz/350g egg noodles
2oz/50g unsalted butter
2 tbsp fresh chives, finely chopped
salt and freshly ground black pepper

Bring a pan of slightly salted boiling water to the boil. Cook noodles until 'al dente', being careful not to overcook. Drain and keep warm. Melt butter in a large saucepan and add chives and seasoning. Stir in noodles and toss gently to coat in buttery mix. Arrange in 'rope' shapes on a warmed serving dish.

Duck with Cherries

Marinated tender duck breast fillets
pan-fried and served with a cherry sauce

SERVES 4

For the marinade
¼ pt/150ml Yellow Label Cabernet
Sauvignon
4 tbsp olive oil
2 cloves garlic, peeled and halved
10 juniper berries
few black peppercorns
1 onion, sliced into rings
1 fresh bay leaf

4 duck breast fillets

For the sauce
½ pt/300ml duck stock (made from breast
bones)
1 glass Yellow Label Cabernet Sauvignon
½ tbsp arrowroot
14oz/400g pitted black cherries, drained
and juice reserved
salt and freshly ground black pepper
½ oz/15g butter, chilled and cut into
small cubes
blanched mangetouts for decoration

Mix marinade ingredients in a large bowl
and add duck breast fillets. Turn to coat
with mixture and leave to soak overnight
or for at least 12 hours. Turn over occasionally. Remove and pat dry. Strain
marinade and reserve any remaining
liquid.

Heat a heavy-bottomed pan and add duck
fillets, skin side down. No oil is necessary
as the duck fat will run. Cook for 7
minutes then turn and fry the other side.
They should still be slightly pink in the
centre. Remove and keep warm while
making the sauce.

Pour off any excess fat from the pan. Pour
duck stock into pan with remaining
marinade and extra wine. Bring to the boil
and simmer gently, skimming off scum,
until slightly reduced. Mix arrowroot to a
paste with 3 tbsp black cherry juice and
stir into sauce. Season and stir until
slightly thickened. Whisk in butter. Pick
out 3 tbsp of the best cherries and add to
sauce. Stir to heat through then keep
sauce warm.

To serve, slice duck into thin slices and
arrange on four warmed serving plates.
Arrange heated mangetouts in a fan shape
underneath then drizzle a little sauce
around meat. Make a little pile of cherries
in the centre to decorate.

Wild Mushroom Stew with Garlic and Pinenuts

Exotic vegetable dish for a special
dinner party

SERVES 4
8oz/225g oyster mushrooms, wiped and
trimmed
8oz/225g chanterelle mushrooms, wiped
and trimmed
1 clove garlic, crushed
2oz/50g unsalted butter
1 tbsp oil
1 tbsp pinenuts, lightly toasted
salt and freshly ground black pepper

Tear mushrooms into pieces. Cook garlic in butter and oil until softened. Add mushrooms and stir fry for 3 minutes. Stir in pinenuts and season with salt and pepper. Pile into a warmed dish and serve with duck and noodles.

34

Wolf Blass's Caesar Salad

Almost a meal in itself, this delicious
salad is crisp and tasty

SERVES 4
2 rashers bacon, de-rinded and grilled
crisp
1 small cos lettuce, washed
1 small iceberg lettuce, washed
1 small head of chicory, washed
12 black olives, stoned
12 cherry tomatoes, wiped and halved
4 sprigs of parsley, snipped into pieces
2 eggs
2 slices white bread, crusts removed and
*   cut into dice*
6 anchovy fillets, chopped

For the dressing
3 tbsp olive oil
5 tbsp white wine vinegar
1 clove garlic, crushed
1 tsp lemon juice
dash Worcester sauce
1 tsp mustard powder
salt and freshly ground black pepper

Cut bacon into strips. Break lettuce and chicory leaves into bite sized pieces. Place in a large bowl with olives, tomatoes, parsley and bacon.

For the dressing whisk all ingredients except eggs in a bowl and pour over salad. Arrange in a serving tureen. Break eggs over salad and gently toss through to coat. Fry bread in a little butter until golden and sprinkle over with anchovy fillets to decorate.

Frozen Coffee Mousses

Light and airy, this is the perfect end
to a sophisticated meal

SERVES 4
4 eggs, separated
4 oz/100g caster sugar
4 tbsp made strong black coffee
1 sachet gelatine
½ pint/300ml double cream, whipped
coffee beans for decoration

Place egg yolks and sugar in a bowl over a pan of simmering water. Whisk until light and creamy and mixture leaves a trail when the whisk is lifted out. Gradually whisk in coffee and remove from heat. Dissolve gelatine in 3 tbsp hot water, cool slightly and stir into egg mixture. Fold in whipped cream and chill until on the point of setting. Whisk egg whites until stiff and carefully fold into mixture. When almost set, pour into individual serving dishes and freeze until firm. Decorate top with coffee beans before serving.

35

LINDEMANS & ROUGE HOMME

WARMING SUPPERS

Wholesome and full-bodied dishes for the cold weather need the rich and flavourful wines of Australia.

Lindemans' red wines are the perfect foil for tasty stews, pies and puddings. Steak, Kidney and Oyster Pudding for example is bliss with the Bin 44 Cabernet Sauvignon – especially if a splash is used in the cooking of the steak and kidney. With a ripe cassis and berry fruit flavour this is an excellent match.

Winter Lamb stew with leeks and carrots is equally delicious with Rouge Homme Cabernet Shiraz, an excitingly plummy and spicy red wine with a distinct touch of class. And with a filling Chicken and Tarragon scone – topped Cobbler, Lindemans' Padthaway Chardonnay, a dry and attractive white wine with a quince and lime scent, is a well-balanced choice.

Rabbit Stew with Onions

*Rabbit, bacon and onions make up the base for this
irresistible substantial stew*

SERVES 4
2 tbsp oil
4 rashers streaky bacon, de-rinded and
    chopped
1 onion, peeled and finely chopped
2 cloves garlic, peeled and crushed
seasoned flour
1 rabbit, jointed
1/4 pint/150ml white wine
1/2 pint/300ml chicken stock
2 sprigs thyme
salt and freshly ground black pepper
12 baby onions, peeled

Heat the oil in a pan and gently fry bacon with onion and garlic over a low heat until the onion has softened. Remove with a slotted spoon and reserve. Dip rabbit joints in flour and add to the pan and fry until browned all over. Return onion mixture to pan, pour over wine and stock and add thyme and seasoning. Bring to the boil, then reduce heat and simmer for 1½ hours or until rabbit is tender. 20 minutes before end of cooking time add baby onions.

Steak, Kidney and Oyster Pudding

A warming favourite, this rich mix of tastes and textures is a wonderful winter feast

SERVES 4

Filling
1 onion, peeled and finely chopped
1 clove garlic, crushed
2 tbsp oil
1 lb/450g chuck steak, cut into neat cubes
seasoned flour
½ wineglass Bin 45 Cabernet Sauvignon
¼ pint/150ml beef stock
3oz/75g smoked oysters (canned)
freshly ground black pepper

Suet pastry
8oz/225g self raising flour
½ tsp salt
6oz/175g shredded suet
10 tbsp cold water

For the filling, cook onion and garlic in oil until softened. Remove with a slotted spoon. Increase heat, add small batches of meat and fry until browned. Return onions to pan and pour over wine and stock. Stir and bring to the boil. Stir in oysters. Season with pepper. Remove from heat.

Sift flour and salt into a bowl. Stir in suet and gradually add water and mix to a firm dough. Knead lightly on a floured surface. Remove one third of the pastry and roll out for a lid. Roll out remaining pastry and line a lightly greased 1½ pint/850ml pudding basin.

Pour filling into suet pastry lined basin. Dampen edges and secure lid on top, sealing well.

Lay a sheet of greaseproof paper on a work surface and cover with a sheet of foil and fold in the centre to make a pleat. Place over basin and tie around the top with string to secure. Trim excess paper. Place in a deep pan one third full of boiling water. Cover and steam for 2½–3 hours, topping up with extra water when necessary.

FOLLOWING PAGES, LEFT TO RIGHT:
Winter Lamb, Steak, Kidney and Oyster Pudding, Chicken and Tarragon Cobbler

Chicken and Tarragon Cobbler

Light but very tasty tarragon flavoured chicken dish
topped with parsley scones for a crust

SERVES 4
4 boned chicken breasts, skinned and cut
into cubes
juice and zest of ½ lemon
2 cloves garlic, peeled and crushed
salt and freshly ground black pepper
2 tbsp oil
1 onion, peeled and finely chopped
4oz/100g tiny button mushrooms, wiped
1oz/25g butter
1 tbsp flour
¼ pint/150ml chicken stock
¼ pint/150ml double cream
1 tbsp fresh tarragon, finely chopped

Herb scone topping
8oz/225g plain flour
2 heaped tsp baking powder
pinch salt
2oz/50g butter
2 tbsp parsley, finely chopped
¼ pint/150ml milk
beaten egg to glaze

Place chicken in a shallow dish and sprinkle with lemon juice and zest and garlic. Season and leave for 30 minutes.

To make the scones, sift flour, baking powder and salt into a bowl. Rub in butter to breadcrumb stage and stir in parsley. Bind with milk to make a soft dough. Knead lightly on a floured board and roll out to ¼in/0.5cm thick. Cut into small rounds with a plain pastry cutter. Cover and chill.

Heat oil and fry onion until softened. Add mushrooms and cook for 2 minutes. Remove with a slotted spoon and reserve. Increase heat and brown chicken pieces.

In a separate pan, melt butter and stir in flour. Cook for 1 minute. Gradually stir in stock and bring to the boil; simmer until slightly thickened. Stir in cream and tarragon. Place chicken and onions in an ovenproof casserole and pour over sauce.

Place scones overlapping around the edge. Brush with beaten egg and place in a preheated oven at Gas 5 375F 190C for 30 minutes or until scones are browned and the chicken is cooked through. Cover with foil if scones become too browned.

Winter Lamb

Simple and delicious casserole dish of lamb flavoured with leeks
and carrots with a hint of rosemary

SERVES 4

2lb/900g boneless lamb, cut into chunks
2 tbsp oil
1 large onion, peeled and finely sliced
1½ pints/850ml lamb stock
2 sprigs rosemary, 1 sprig parsley and
*   bay leaf tied with string*
salt and freshly ground black pepper
1lb/450g potatoes, peeled and cut into
*   chunks*
3 leeks, washed and sliced
1 parsnip, peeled and chopped
2 carrots, peeled and sliced

Fry lamb in oil until browned. Place in an ovenproof casserole. Gently fry onion until softened and add to lamb. Pour over stock and add herbs and seasoning. Cover and cook in a preheated oven for 1 hour at Gas 4 350F 180C. Stir in vegetables and return to the oven for a further hour or until vegetables and meat are tender.

Duck Casserole with Olives

An easy-going kind of casserole – but at the same time made
from ingredients smart enough to lift it into the dinner party repertoire

SERVES 4

For the marinade
1 onion, peeled and roughly chopped
2 cloves garlic, crushed
1 wineglass red wine
3 tbsp fruity olive oil
3 tbsp brine from olive jar
2 bay leaves
sprig of fresh thyme
few black peppercorns, lightly crushed
1 ovenready duck, jointed

1 Spanish onion, peeled and finely
*   chopped*
2 tbsp oil
¾ pint/425ml duck or chicken stock
fresh bouquet garni
salt and freshly ground black pepper
12 stoned black olives

Put marinade ingredients into a bowl and mix thoroughly. Add duck joints and spoon marinade over to coat. Leave overnight, turning occasionally. Remove duck and strain marinade, reserving liquid. Pat duck dry with kitchen paper.

Fry onion in oil until soft, remove with a slotted spoon and reserve. Add duck joints and brown on all sides. Remove any excess fat that runs from the duck. Add marinade, stock and herbs. Bring to the boil. Season with salt and pepper. Transfer with onions to an ovenproof casserole. Cover and cook in a preheated oven at Gas 3 325F 160C for 1½ hours or until the duck is tender. Add olives 5 minutes before end of cooking time.

TYRRELL'S

ITALIAN STYLE

Just about everyone's favourite food includes something Italian. This colourful and satisfying cuisine has the complete appeal of the perfect meal. And to drink with it? Try Australian wines. Tyrrell's range is particularly appropriate.
The delicious flavours of a scorched fennel salad, for example, are well-matched by the Semillon Sauvignon Blanc, a grassy tasting wine with a delicate fruity nose. The rich stew Osso Buco, made with shin of veal in tomato and white wine sauce with a saffron risotto, tastes even better with the smooth, brambly blackcurrant fruit of the Cabernet Sauvignon Merlot.
And the perfect wine to serve with the famous Italian blue cheese, Gorgonzola, is Tyrrell's Pinot Noir. This lovely wine is lightly scented, with a soft and delicate hint of strawberries in the taste.

CLOCKWISE FROM TOP LEFT:
Scorched Fennel Salad, Saffron Risotto, Osso Buco

Osso Buco

Traditional Italian favourite of shin of veal with the marrow in, slowly cooked in tomato, white wine and stock, flavoured with parsley and lemon

SERVES 4
4 large pieces of shin of veal
seasoned flour
2 tbsp oil
1oz/25g butter
1 onion, peeled and finely chopped
2 trimmed stalks from a fennel bulb,
  finely sliced
½ pint/300ml dry white wine
½ pint/300ml chicken stock
2 tomatoes, skinned and chopped
salt and freshly ground black pepper
zest and juice of 1 lemon
1 clove garlic, crushed
1tbsp parsley, finely chopped
extra lemon zest and fennel fronds for
  decoration

Dip veal in seasoned flour to coat lightly. Heat oil and butter in a pan and fry onion and fennel until softened. Remove with a slotted spoon, and reserve.

Add veal to pan and brown on all sides. Return onion mix to pan and pour over wine and stock. Add tomatoes, and season with salt and pepper. Cover with a tight fitting lid and simmer for 1½–2 hours, or until veal is tender. Five minutes before end of cooking time add lemon zest and juice, garlic and parsley. Serve veal with a little of the sauce spooned over. Sprinkle over a little lemon zest and decorate with a frond of fennel. Serve with Saffron Risotto.

Saffron Risotto

Amber coloured and fragrant risotto which is the perfect accompaniment to Osso Buco

SERVES 4
1 onion, peeled and finely chopped
1 clove garlic, crushed
1 tbsp oil
½ tsp saffron powder
8oz/225g Arborio rice
1½ pints/850ml vegetable stock
salt and freshly ground black pepper
1oz/25g butter
2 tbsp freshly grated Parmesan

Cook onion and garlic in oil until soft. Stir in saffron powder and rice and mix well. Add a little stock, and when this is absorbed add a little more, cooking until the rice is tender. Season, and stir in butter. Spoon into a serving dish and sprinkle over cheese.

Scorched Fennel Salad

Spectacular first course of sliced scorched fennel, interleaved with beef tomatoes, and slices of mozzarella and avocado with a light olive oil dressing

SERVES 4

2 fennel bulbs, trimmed
2 tbsp oil
1 clove garlic, crushed
2 beef tomatoes
6oz/175g mozzarella
1 avocado
lemon juice
basil sprigs for decoration

Dressing
3 tbsp olive oil
1 tbsp white wine vinegar
pinch sugar
squeeze of lemon juice
salt and freshly ground black pepper

Thinly slice fennel bulbs vertically. Heat oil and garlic and fry fennel slices over a high heat until browned. Remove and drain on kitchen paper. Season and leave to cool.

Arrange fennel slices around a large serving platter. Interleave tomato and mozzarella slices in the centre. Halve, peel and stone avocado. Sprinkle with lemon juice and thinly slice lengthways and press lightly to fan out. Arrange in the centre of platter. Shake dressing ingredients and drizzle over and decorate with basil sprigs.

45

Warm Courgette Salad with Pinenuts

Courgette sticks gently sautéed with pinenuts and rosemary

SERVES 4

4 tbsp olive oil
4 large courgettes, trimmed, washed and
    cut into sticks
2 tbsp toasted pinenuts
1 tsp rosemary, chopped
salt and freshly ground black pepper

Heat oil in a pan and gently fry courgettes until just cooked but still crisp. Stir in pinenuts and rosemary and season with salt and pepper. Turn into a dish and serve warm.

Pizza Passion

Nothing beats a home made pizza – especially with
liberal amounts of your favourite topping

Pizza dough
1 tsp sugar
¼ pint/150ml warm water
1 tsp dried yeast
8oz/225g strong plain flour
½ tsp salt
½ oz/15g butter

Tomato sauce base for one pizza
1 tbsp olive oil
1 small onion, peeled and finely chopped
1 clove garlic, crushed
1 tbsp tomato purée
6 tomatoes, peeled, deseeded and chopped
¼ pint/150ml vegetable stock
salt and freshly ground black pepper

Salami, black olive &
mozzarella topping
8 thin slices pepper salami
8 stoned black olives
4oz/100g thin sliced mozzarella cheese

Onion and mushroom topping
1 Spanish onion, peeled and finely sliced
2 cloves garlic
2 tbsp olive oil
1 tsp fresh oregano
1 tsp sugar
8oz/225g button mushrooms, wiped and
sliced
salt and freshly ground black pepper
2oz/50g grated mozzarella

Four-cheese pizza
Choose four contrasting flavours or
colours of cheese

3oz/75g Cheddar cheese, grated
3oz/75g blue cheese, crumbled
3oz/75g Brie, de-rinded and thinly sliced
3oz/75g Gruyère, grated
3oz/75g tin anchovies, drained
olive oil for sprinkling
2 tsp marjoram, chopped
freshly ground black pepper

To make the pizza dough, dissolve sugar
in water. Sprinkle yeast over and leave in a
warm place for 10 minutes until frothy.
Sift flour and salt into a bowl, rub in
butter, and pour in yeast liquid. Mix to a
soft dough and knead on a lightly floured
surface. Sprinkle a little flour into a bowl,
and put dough in. Cover and stand bowl in
a roasting tin half filled with hot water.
Leave in a warm place to double in size.

Roll out dough to a 10″/25cm circle and
place on greased baking tray.

For tomato base, heat oil and fry onion
and garlic until softened. Stir in tomato
purée and tomatoes and cook for 5
minutes. Pour in stock and season. Simmer until reduced and slightly thickened.
Spread over pizza dough.

For salami pizza, lay salami slices on top
of dough, spread with tomato sauce, dot
with olives and cover with cheese.

For onion and mushroom topping, fry
onion and garlic in oil until softened. Stir
in oregano, sugar and mushrooms and
cook for 2 minutes. Season. Spread
tomato sauce over pizza dough and pile
onion mix on top. Sprinkle with cheese.

For four-cheese pizza, sprinkle each
cheese into neat triangles on tomato-
topped dough and edge with anchovies to
form a cartwheel design. Sprinkle with
olive oil, marjoram and pepper.

Bake in a preheated oven at Gas 6 400F
200C for 25 minutes.

Peaches Puccini

*Fresh peaches with a nut stuffing, served with
a Zabaglione sauce*

SERVES 4

4 ripe peaches
4oz/100g butter, softened
4oz/100g icing sugar
2 tbsp chopped almonds, toasted
3 tbsp Amaretto

Zabaglione sauce

4 eggs
4 tsp sugar
4 fl oz/100ml Marsala

Cut lid from top of each peach, and cut a thin slice from the base to balance fruit on the plate. With a teaspoon, carefully scoop out the stones. Mix remaining ingredients and stuff into the hollows of each peach.

For the sauce, place eggs and sugar in a bowl over a pan of simmering water and whisk until pale, thick and frothy, gradually adding Marsala.

Pour a little sauce onto 4 individual serving plates and sit a peach in the centre.

DEJEUNER SUR L'HERBE

Eating in the fresh air has a way of making food taste even more delicious – especially accompanied by excellent Australian wines. Hardy's Grand Reserve Sparkling Wine, both Brut and Rosé are fragrant, refreshing and fruity, the superb summer drink for indoor and outdoor occasions – a natural choice for the perfect picnic.

Excite the appetite with a boned chicken stuffed with tasty mix of rice, fruit and nuts – and a bottle of the Hardy Collection Chardonnay, a full-bodied dry white wine with a hint of limes in the fruit.

A blue cheese quiche is subtly flavoured and creamy and well-matched by Hardy's Cabernet Sauvignon Shiraz, a spicy red wine.

Ascot Chicken

Whole boned chicken – ask your butcher to do this – with a stuffing of nuts, apricots and mushrooms. Serve this in easy to cut slices

SERVES 6
For the stuffing
2 tbsp oil
2 cloves garlic, crushed
1 onion, peeled and finely chopped
1 lb/450g mushrooms, wiped and finely chopped
3 tbsp finely chopped parsley
2 tbsp dry white wine
3 oz/75g walnuts, finely chopped
3 oz/75g no soak apricots, snipped into small pieces
10 oz/275g cooked long grain rice
salt and freshly ground black pepper

3 lb/1.6kg chicken, boned
oil for brushing
tomatoes, parsley and watercress for decoration

Heat oil in a pan and fry garlic and onion until softened. Add mushrooms, parsley and wine and stir over a low heat for 3 minutes. Spoon into a bowl and stir in walnuts, apricots, rice and seasoning. Mix well and leave to cool.

Wipe chicken inside and out and stuff cavity and legs with stuffing mixture. Truss chicken to retain shape during cooking.

Place on a wire rack and brush chicken with oil. Season with salt and pepper and roast in a preheated oven at Gas 6 400F 200C for 20 minutes per 1 lb/450g, plus 20 minutes or until juices run clear when pierced with a skewer. Remove from oven and leave to cool completely. Place on a serving platter and decorate with tomatoes, parsley and watercress. Serve in slices.

Blue Cheese Quiche

The combination of the traditional quiche mixture with a filling of blue cheese is paradise on earth

SERVES 6
8 oz/225g wholemeal shortcrust pastry
6 oz/175g Gorgonzola cheese, crumbled
2 eggs, beaten
¼ pint/150ml milk
4 tbsp double cream
freshly ground black pepper

Roll out pastry on a lightly floured board to fit an 8in/20cm fluted quiche dish. Chill pastry for 30 minutes.

Sprinkle cheese over pastry base. Mix eggs, milk, cream and seasoning and pour over cheese. Bake in a preheated oven at Gas 6 400F 200C for 35 minutes or until mixture has set.

FOLLOWING PAGES, CLOCKWISE FROM TOP LEFT:
Ascot Chicken, Melon Baskets, Salade Marseillaise, Blue Cheese Quiche

Salade Marseillaise

*Fresh tasting mixed salad of cold cooked white fish with tomatoes, lettuce,
French beans, new potatoes and black olives dressed with vinaigrette*

SERVES 4
1 lb/450g cod fillet, poached and cooled
6 oz/175g cherry tomatoes
1 frisée lettuce, washed
6 oakleaf lettuce leaves, washed
4 oz/100g French beans, blanched and
    cut into short lengths
12 stoned black olives, cut into quarters
12 new potatoes, peeled and cooked

Garlic dressing
4 tbsp sunflower oil
2 tbsp olive oil
2 tbsp white wine vinegar
3 cloves garlic, crushed
zest and squeeze of ½ lemon
1 tsp Dijon mustard
salt and freshly ground black pepper

Flake fish into large pieces, and cut
tomatoes in half. Tear salad leaves into
bite size pieces and place in a serving bowl
with beans, olives and potatoes. Arrange
fish flakes amongst salad leaves. Shake
dressing ingredients in a screwtop jar, and
pour over salad just before serving.

Chilled Parsley and Potato Soup

Deep green and utterly luscious herby soup

SERVES 4
1 oz/25g butter
1 onion, peeled and finely chopped
1 clove garlic, crushed
1½ pints/850ml vegetable stock
2 potatoes, peeled and roughly
    chopped
3 tbsp parsley, finely chopped
¼ pint/150ml double cream
salt and freshly ground black pepper

Heat butter and oil in a pan and fry onion
and garlic until softened. Pour over stock
and add potatoes and parsley. Bring to the
boil and simmer until potatoes are tender.
Place in a blender and whizz until
smooth. Return to a bowl and gradually
stir in cream. Season with salt and pepper,
cover and leave to cool.
Serve sprinkled with a little finely chopped parsley.

Aubergine Purée

A robust dip made from roasted aubergines
with garlic and chives

SERVES 4
2 aubergines, cut in half and the flesh
scored
salt and freshly ground black pepper
4 cloves garlic, crushed
1 tbsp snipped chives
¼ pint/150ml olive oil

Place aubergines on a baking sheet, brush with a little oil and season with salt and pepper. Wrap in foil and bake at Gas 6 400F 200C for 30 minutes.

Remove from oven and scoop out flesh and mash. Stir in garlic and chives. Beat in oil a little at a time until blended and smooth. Spoon into a pot and serve with warmed pitta bread cut in strips.

53

Melon Cups

Halved Ogen melons with a filling of fresh fruit
topped with sparkling wine

SERVES 4
2 Ogen melons, halved and pips removed
8 oz/225g strawberries, hulled
6 oz/175g black grapes, halved and pipped
8 tbsp sparkling white wine

Scoop the flesh from each melon half into balls with a melon baller. Tidy up the shells. Arrange melon balls, strawberries and grapes in melon shells and pour over wine. Chill and serve.

ROSEMOUNT ESTATE

SENSATIONAL SEAFOOD

From prawns to oysters, sole to salmon, mussels to monkfish – the sea yields the most delectable array of tastes and textures.

Nothing accompanies fish better than wines of Australia.

Savour the idea of a rich fish soup crammed with chunks of fish and shellfish with a bottle of Rosemount Hunter Valley Shiraz. This medium-bodied dry red wine is lightly aged in French oak casks to produce a spicy, peppery red which is a perfect match.

London Lobster is a simple but sophisticated way of serving this luxury crustacean with an unusual gin and spring onion flavoured sauce. Rosemount White's Creek Semillon is the best choice with this dish. Rich, full and fruity with a crisp balance of acidity, this wine is the perfect complement.

The Rosemount Chardonnay also lends itself to fish dishes – amongst many others. Full and rich with a touch of oak, this is a fruity, dry white wine.

Oysters Gratinée

*Rather a special dish of oysters topped with seasoned
breadcrumbs and grilled*

SERVES 4
24 oysters
6 tbsp fish stock
wine glass of dry white wine
freshly ground black pepper
1 egg yolk
6 tbsp double cream
2 tbsp fresh white breadcrumbs

Open oysters over a bowl to catch juice.
Remove oysters from shells and place in a

pan with strained juice, stock and wine.
Season with pepper and poach for about
15–20 seconds. Remove with a slotted
spoon. Replace in cleaned half shells.

Bring liquid in the pan to the boil until
reduced by a third. Remove from heat,
whisk in egg yolk and cream. Spoon a
little cream sauce over each oyster and
sprinkle with a few breadcrumbs. Flash
under a hot grill to brown.

55

Sole Fillets with Prawn Mousse

*Luxury dinner party dish of sole fillets encasing
a mousse of prawns*

SERVES 4
For the mousse
2 sole fillets
3 egg whites
8oz/225g peeled prawns
½ pint/300ml double cream
1 tbsp dill
salt and freshly ground white pepper

2 soles, filleted and skinned
6 tbsp fish stock
4 tbsp dry white wine

Place sole in blender and whizz with egg
whites until smooth. Finely chop prawns,
and whisk cream until fairly thick. Fold
into fish mixture. Stir in dill and season
with salt and pepper.

Place sole fillets on a flat surface. Liberally
spread prawn mousse along the length.
Roll up each sole neatly and secure with a
cocktail stick. Place in a shallow ovenproof dish and spoon over stock and wine.
Season, cover and bake in a preheated
oven at Gas 5 375F 190C for 15–20
minutes or until fish is cooked.

Mediterranean Salad

Chunky fish salad with peppers and spring onion.
Utterly delicious with a dill vinaigrette

SERVES 4

1 lb/450g thick cod fillet
1 lb/450g monkfish, boned, trimmed, and
  cut into chunks
1/4 pint/150ml fish stock
1 squid, cleaned, sliced into rings, plus
  tentacles
2 tbsp oil
1 clove garlic
4 oz/100g prawns
2 oz/50g shrimps
1 small red and green pepper, de-seeded
  and cut into tiny squares
4 spring onions, trimmed and thinly
  sliced

Dill vinaigrette
6 tbsp sunflower oil
2 tbsp dill vinegar
juice of 1/2 lime
1 tsp Dijon mustard
1 tbsp dill, finely chopped
salt and freshly ground black pepper
sprig of dill for decoration

Poach cod and monkfish in fish stock. Remove with a slotted spoon and leave to cool. Flake cod and remove any bones.

Pat squid dry on kitchen paper. Heat oil and garlic in a pan and add squid rings and tentacles. Flash fry for about 1 minute or until opaque. Cool. Do not overcook.

Arrange fish in a serving dish with squid, prawns, shrimps, peppers and spring onions. Whisk dressing ingredients in a bowl and drizzle over salad; lightly toss to coat. Decorate with a sprig of dill.

London Lobster

Lobster served with a gin mayonnaise. If the lobsters are small, serve one each, otherwise half a large one will be enough. Remember the lobster crackers and picks.

SERVES 4

2 large cooked lobsters about 1 1/2 lb/700g
  each

For the sauce
1 egg yolk
1 tsp Dijon mustard
1/4 pint/150ml sunflower oil
2 tsp garlic vinegar
1 tbsp gin
1 tbsp spring onions, finely chopped

Beat egg yolk with mustard. Add oil drip by drip, beating well to make sure it is all incorporated before the next drop is added. As soon as the mixture begins to emulsify add oil in a very thin stream, still beating vigorously until all oil is used up.

Beat in vinegar and gin, then stir in spring onions. Spoon into a serving pot and serve with lobsters.

Fish Soup

*Russet coloured, rich-tasting soup with chunks of fish
and shellfish – a meal in itself*

SERVES 4
12 oz/350g hake, skinned and filleted
12 oz/350g salmon, skinned and filleted
1 pint/600ml fresh mussels
¼ pint/150ml white wine
4 tbsp olive oil
1 large onion, peeled and finely chopped
2 cloves garlic, crushed
*½ bulb fennel, trimmed and finely
  chopped*
1 tbsp tomato purée
2 pints/1.1 litre fish stock
fresh bouquet garni
seasoned flour
1 pint/600ml prawns
salt and freshly ground black pepper
1 tbsp finely chopped parsley

Wipe fish and cut into chunks. Scrub and debeard mussels, discarding any that do not open when tapped with the back of a knife. Bring wine to the boil in a large pan and add mussels. Cover and steam until open. Strain and reserve cooking liquid and discard mussels that are still closed.

Heat oil in a large pan and cook onion, garlic and fennel until softened. Stir in tomato purée and stock. Add bouquet garni and bring to the boil. Dip fish in flour and add to pan with reserved mussels and cooking liquid and prawns. Simmer until fish is cooked through, season and spoon into warmed bowls. Sprinkle with parsley to serve.

57

Grilled Salmon Steaks

*Simple but delicious, these salmon steaks are perfumed
with fresh tarragon*

SERVES 4
4 salmon steaks, about 1"/2.5cm thick
4 oz/100g butter
juice and zest of 1 lemon
salt and freshly ground black pepper
1 tbsp tarragon, finely chopped
*lemon slices and tarragon sprigs to
  decorate*

Wipe salmon and place on baking sheet lined with tin foil. Dot the steaks with half the butter, drizzle with half lemon juice and zest and sprinkle with half the tarragon. Season.

Grill fish under a preheated grill for 5 minutes then turn over, dot with remaining butter, pour over remaining lemon juice and zest and sprinkle with remaining tarragon. Continue grilling for a further 5 minutes or until cooked through. The fish is done when it becomes opaque and the bone is easily removed. Serve on individual plates decorated with tarragon and lemon slices.

FOLLOWING PAGES, LEFT TO RIGHT:
*London Lobster, Fish Soup,
Mediterranean Salad*

WYNDHAM ESTATE

TASTE OF
THE EAST

Spicy oriental foods lend themselves to the varied flavours of the wines of Australia. A spread of dishes from south-east Asia, for example, is well-accompanied by a selection of wines from Wyndham Estate. Beef Satay with a Peanut Sauce is suited by the smooth blackcurrant and brambly flavours of Wyndham Estate Bin 444. Chicken Curry with Basil with its distinct south-east Asian taste teams with the Hunter Valley Chardonnay with its soft, buttery style and crisp, clean fragrance. Even a highly flavoured and spiced squid dish with garlic, red and green peppers and soy sauce is enhanced by a bottle of Bin 333 Pinot Noir. The floral bouquet and delicate raspberry fruit match well. And drink a glass of Wyndham Estate Oak Cask Chardonnay with a simple dish of pan-fried prawns with garlic, ginger and chilli.

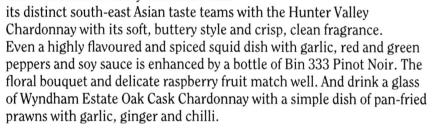

FOLLOWING PAGES, CLOCKWISE FROM TOP LEFT:
Squid with Garlic and Peppers, Fried Noodles, Beef Satay with Peanut Sauce, Chicken Curry with Basil, Chilli Prawns

Beef Satay with Peanut Sauce

*Little skewers of lean beef marinated to delicious tenderness
and served with a spicy peanut sauce*

SERVES 4
For the beef marinade
2 tbsp oil
1 onion, peeled and chopped
juice of 1 lime
few sprigs coriander
2 cloves garlic
1 tbsp soy sauce
1 tsp root ginger, grated

4 thin slices lean rump steak, cut into
small cubes

For the sauce
6 tbsp desiccated coconut
8floz/225ml boiling water
5 tbsp crunchy peanut butter
1 tbsp oil
2 cloves garlic, peeled and crushed
½ tsp chilli sauce
1 tbsp soy sauce

For the marinade, place all ingredients except steak in a blender and purée until almost smooth. Thread steak cubes onto wooden skewers and place in a shallow dish. Spread marinade purée over, cover and leave to soak for at least 12 hours or preferably overnight.

For the sauce, mix coconut and water and leave to stand for 30 minutes. Stir well, then strain, reserving liquid and discarding coconut. Mix with peanut butter. Heat oil in a pan and gently fry garlic. Stir in peanut butter mixture, chilli sauce and soy sauce. Stir over a low heat until thickened.

Grill beef skewers until browned and cooked through. Arrange on a platter and decorate with lime wedges and coriander sprigs. Spoon sauce into a pot and serve with beef.

Fried Chilli Prawns

*Scrumptious large prawns cooked simply with ginger,
chilli, garlic and lemon*

SERVES 4
12 Mediterranean prawns
3 tbsp oil
1 tsp root ginger, grated
2 red chillies, deseeded and finely
chopped
2 cloves garlic, crushed
juice of ½ lemon
salt and freshly ground black pepper
lemon twist and sprig of parsley to
decorate

Remove heads from prawns and carefully peel off tail shells. Heat oil in a pan and gently cook ginger, chillies and garlic until softened. Add prawns and stir fry for 3 minutes or until hot. Sprinkle over lemon juice and season with salt and pepper. Arrange on a pretty plate and decorate with a lemon twist and a sprig of continental parsley.

Chicken Curry with Basil

Delicate white meat of chicken breast in strips flavoured with basil, chilli and cumin to make a dainty curry with a thin sauce of coconut cream

SERVES 4

4 chicken breast fillets, skinned and cut
   into strips
2 tbsp oil
1 onion, peeled and finely chopped
½ tsp cumin
½ tsp turmeric
1 tsp chilli powder
3 tbsp coconut cream
¾ pint/425ml boiling water
salt and freshly ground black pepper
few basil leaves, shredded
basil sprigs to decorate

Fry chicken in oil until browned. Remove with a slotted spoon and reserve. Add onion to pan and cook gently until softened, using a little more oil if necessary. Stir in spices and cook for a further minute. Return chicken to pan and stir to coat with onion mix.

Mix coconut cream with water and pour over chicken. Season with salt and pepper and bring to the boil. Gently simmer until chicken is cooked through, topping up with more water if necessary. Stir in shredded basil and spoon into a serving bowl. Decorate with basil sprigs just before serving.

Squid with Garlic and Peppers

Squid rings and chopped tentacles cooked with garlic, peppers and soy sauce. Be sure not to overcook

SERVES 4

1 fresh squid, cleaned
3 tbsp oil
4 cloves garlic, peeled and crushed
1 red pepper and 1 green pepper,
   de-seeded and cut into strips
good dash of soy sauce
salt and freshly ground black pepper

Cut the body of the squid into rings and chop the tentacles. Heat oil in a large pan and cook garlic and peppers until softened. Add squid pieces and cook for 6 minutes, stirring. Season with soy sauce and salt and pepper. Arrange on a warm plate and serve immediately.

Fried Noodles

*A dish on its own or the perfect accompaniment
to all the others – egg noodles flecked with
tiny nuggets of onions, peppers and garlic*

SERVES 4
12oz/375g egg noodles
2 tbsp sesame oil
1 onion, peeled and finely chopped
2 cloves garlic, peeled and crushed
1 small red and 1 small green pepper,
   de-seeded and finely diced
good dash of soy sauce
freshly ground pepper

Blanch noodles in lightly salted boiling water. Drain. Heat oil in a pan and gently cook onion and garlic until softened. Add peppers and stir fry for 2 minutes. Stir in noodles and toss through to mix with vegetables. Season with soy sauce and pepper. Pile onto a plate and serve as an accompaniment.

65

Spicy Pork-Stuffed Omelette

*A thick herb-flavoured omelette gently
spiced and filled with pork and peas*

SERVES 1
Filling
1 tbsp oil
1 clove garlic, crushed
1 tsp grated root ginger
½ red chilli, deseeded and finely chopped
zest of ½ lemon
few coriander seeds, crushed
3oz/75g minced pork
1 tsp oyster sauce
1 tbsp cooked peas
freshly ground black pepper

Omelette
2 eggs
1 tbsp milk
1 tsp fresh coriander, finely chopped
salt and freshly ground black pepper

Heat oil in a pan and gently fry garlic, root ginger and chilli until softened. Stir in lemon zest and coriander seeds with minced pork. Fry over a high heat until pork browns and is cooked through. Stir in oyster sauce and peas and heat through. Season with pepper and keep filling hot whilst making omelette.

Mix eggs, milk, coriander and seasoning. Heat a little oil in an omelette pan and pour in egg mixture. Stir mixture with a fork from the edge to the middle until it has set. Spoon pork mixture over one side and fold over omelette. Slide on to a warmed serving plate.

BROWN BROTHERS
GRAND FINALE

There is nothing to beat Australia's dessert wines. They are what puddings were invented for – especially the astounding range of sweet wines from Brown Brothers. Brown Brothers late harvest Orange Muscat and Flora is uniquely honey and fruit-scented with hints of orange blossom. It has a delicious rich grapey taste with a clean fresh finish – the perfect partner to Boodles Orange Fool – or any other fruity dessert. The glorious Dessert Muscat is rich and raisiny – and good with a Chocolate Roulade. The late picked Muscat Blanc with its enticing spicy nose and mouth-filling grapey taste is an excellent match for the Grape Tart. Brown Brothers Noble Riesling is a delightful golden colour with hints of toffee and honey on the nose. It makes a wonderful accompaniment to many desserts – and also cheese and fruity platters. And the Reserve Tawny with its chocolatey scent and subtle fruit is a good choice with cheese.

66

FROM TOP TO BOTTOM:
Gâteau St. Honoré, Chocolate Roulade, Grape Tart

Chocolate Roulade

Luxurious light and airy chocolate roll
filled with whipped cream

SERVES 6
5 eggs
6oz/175g caster sugar
6oz/175g dark chocolate
1/2 pint/300ml double cream, whipped
icing sugar, sifted
whipped cream and chocolate caraque
for decoration

Separate eggs and whisk yolks and sugar until thick and creamy. Melt chocolate in a bowl over a pan of simmering water, cool slightly then stir into yolk mixture. Whisk egg whites until stiff, and carefully fold into mixture.

Line a Swiss roll tin with lightly buttered greaseproof paper. Pour in mixture and spread evenly. Bake in a preheated oven at Gas 5 375F 190C for 30 minutes or until just firm to the touch. Cool and turn out onto greaseproof paper sprinkled with icing sugar. Leave to cool. Spread over cream, allowing a 1"/2.5cm gap along the long sides. Roll up carefully and sprinkle over icing sugar. Decorate with whipped cream swirls and chocolate caraque.

Grape Tart

Crisp puff pastry base topped with cream and
diagonal lines of green and black grapes

SERVES 6
Pastry
12oz/350g puff pastry
1 egg yolk, beaten

Filling
1/2 pint/300ml double cream
1 tbsp Brown Brothers Late Picked Muscat
6oz/175g seedless white grapes
6oz/175g seedless black grapes
apricot jam
lemon juice

Roll out pastry on a lightly floured board into an oblong. Cut a neat 1/2"/1cm border from around the edge. Roll the inner oblong out by 1/2"/1cm to measure the same size again. Neatly attach the border to the base with a little beaten egg. Chill for 30 minutes. Glaze with egg, prick the base and bake in a preheated oven at Gas 7 425F 220C until golden and risen. Remove and cool on a wire rack.

Whip cream with Muscat and spread into base of pastry case. Halve grapes and arrange in alternate diagonal lines. Melt apricot jam with lemon juice and sieve. Brush over grapes to glaze.

Gâteau St Honoré

Choux pastry gâteau topped with spun sugar

SERVES 6

Pastry base
4oz/100g flour
pinch salt
1oz/25g butter
1oz/25g lard
iced water

Choux pastry
1/2 pint/300ml milk and water mixed
4oz/100g butter
5oz/150g plain flour sifted with a pinch of salt
4 small eggs, beaten

Pastry cream
2 eggs
2oz/50g sugar
1oz/25g plain flour
1/2 pint/300ml milk
vanilla pod

Sugar syrup for spun sugar
4oz/100g granulated sugar
2 fl oz/50ml water

1 punnet strawberries, wiped and hulled

For pastry base, sift flour and salt into a bowl. Rub in fat to breadcrumb stage. Mix to a dough with water, knead lightly then roll out to a 7"/18cm circle. Place on a greased baking sheet and chill.

For choux, put milk, water and butter in a pan and bring to the boil. Add flour and beat until mixture leaves the sides of the pan. Remove from heat and cool slightly. Add eggs a little at a time, beating in between until mix is glossy. Spoon into a piping bag fitted with a plain nozzle and pipe a ring of choux around the edge of the shortcrust base. Pipe remaining choux into small buns on a separate baking sheet.

Bake at Gas 6 400F 200C for 10 minutes. Reduce heat to Gas 4 350F 180C and cook until golden and crisp. The pastry case may need a little longer than the buns. Cool.

For pastry cream, whisk eggs and sugar until creamy. Whisk in flour. Bring milk almost to the boil, with the vanilla pod, then remove pod and gradually pour into egg mixture, stirring. Pour back into the pan and stir over a low heat until thickened. Cool and cover with buttered greaseproof paper until needed. Spread pastry cream in the base of pastry case.

Dissolve the sugar in water in a pan. Bring to the boil until just golden.

Carefully dip the base of the choux buns into the caramel and stick around the pastry case. Arrange strawberries in the centre on top of pastry cream.

Dip a fork into remaining caramel and trail threads of spun sugar over the cake. Serve immediately.

Treacle Tart

An old-fashioned favourite

SERVES 4
6oz/175g plain flour, sifted with a pinch of salt
3oz/75g butter
2–3 tbsp iced water

Filling
8fl oz/200ml golden syrup
juice and grated rind of a lemon
good grating of nutmeg
8 tbsp fresh white breadcrumbs
2 tbsp soured cream

Sift flour into a bowl and rub in butter to breadcrumb stage. Add water and mix to a soft dough. Knead lightly, roll out and line an 8"/20cm flan tin. Chill 30 minutes.

Warm syrup, lemon juice, rind and nutmeg in a pan. Remove from heat and stir in breadcrumbs and soured cream. Pour into pastry case and bake in a preheated oven at Gas 7 425F 220C for 20 minutes until pastry is golden brown.

Lemon Cheesecake

Utterly irresistible classic baked creamy cheesecake

SERVES 8
6oz/175g Digestive biscuits, crushed
1 tsp cinnamon
good grating fresh nutmeg
4oz/100g butter, melted
1½ lb/700g cream cheese
¼ pt/150ml soured cream
2oz/50g sugar
4 eggs
juice of half a lemon

Mix biscuit crumbs, cinnamon and nutmeg with butter and press into the base of an 8"/20cm loose-bottomed cake tin.

Beat cream cheese smooth with the soured cream. Add sugar. Beat in the eggs one at a time. Stir in lemon juice. Pour mixture over crumb base and smooth over the top.

Bake in a pre-heated oven Gas 5 375F 190C for about 45 minutes – or until top is firm. Leave for 5 minutes in the tin, then carefully remove and leave to cool.

Boodles Orange Fool

Famous pudding from Boodles Club in St.
James Street, London, founded in 1764

SERVES 4
1 large plain sponge cake
4 tbsp dry sherry
juice of 4 oranges
juice of 2 lemons
zest of 2 oranges and 1 lemon
1 pint/600ml double cream
1 tbsp caster sugar
julienne strips of orange rind
¼ pint/150ml cream, whipped, and
orange pieces for decoration

Cut sponge cake into small pieces and place in the base of a trifle bowl. Sprinkle over sherry. Whisk orange, lemon juice and zest, cream and caster sugar together. Pour over sponge cakes. Chill for at least 2 hours. Just before serving decorate with orange strips, swirls of whipped cream and orange pieces.

DRINKS PARTY

Take advantage of Orlando's range of wines to accompany canapés at a drinks party. Nothing gets a party off to a good start better than a glass of sparkling wine – so chill plenty of the yeasty, creamy, fruity Orlando Carrington Extra Brut in anticipation. Then a choice of reds and whites will please every guest.

Jacob's Creek Dry Red is a soft, fruity wine with immense appeal, made from the grapes Shiraz, Cabernet Sauvignon and Malbec. The Medium Dry White has a clean fresh fragrance with lingering fruit flavours, perfect with bite-sized nibbles.

Orlando's RF Sauvignon Blanc has elegance for the more sophisticated palates which will enjoy its distinct herby fruit and crisp acidity.

Or serve the richly scented and oaky red, Orlando St. Hugo, or the fragrant and smoky St. Hilary with its attractive, rounded Chardonnay fruit.

FOLLOWING PAGES CLOCKWISE FROM TOP LEFT:
Quail's Eggs with Dipping Salts, Chicken Twizzles, Garlic Mussels, Stuffed Cherry Tomatoes, Crostini.

Crostini

Thin slices of toasted French bread drizzled with olive oil,
spread with a choice of savoury toppings

SERVES 10
2 French sticks cut on the slant into
½"/1cm slices
olive oil

Green olive topping
8oz/225g stoned green olives, finely
chopped

Fresh tomato and basil topping
6 tomatoes, skinned, deseeded and diced
few basil leaves, shredded
salt and freshly ground black pepper

Chicken liver topping
8oz/225g chicken livers, washed and
picked over to remove gristle
1 clove garlic, crushed
1 shallot, peeled and finely chopped
2oz/50g butter
1 tbsp brandy
salt and freshly ground black pepper

Fresh garlic topping
1 bulb of garlic, cloves peeled, and crushed
salt

Toast bread slices both sides and drizzle with oil.

Spread olive topping onto a few bread slices.

For fresh tomato and basil topping, mix tomato and basil. Season with salt and pepper and spread on bread slices.

For chicken liver topping, fry livers with garlic in butter until browned. Flame with brandy and season with salt and pepper. Roughly blend in a processor and spread on to bread slices.

For garlic topping, grind cloves with salt in a pestle and mortar. Spread onto bread slices and drizzle with a little extra oil.

Arrange on a serving platter.

Stuffed Cherry Tomatoes

Whole cherry tomatoes with the seeds removed and
replaced with nutty stuffing

SERVES 10
1 punnet cherry tomatoes (approx 20)

For the stuffing
3 tbsp oil
1 small onion, peeled and finely chopped
2 cloves garlic, peeled and crushed
2 tbsp fresh white breadcrumbs
2oz/50g ground almonds
1 tbsp fresh parsley, chopped
salt and freshly ground black pepper

Leaving the calyx on each tomato, cut a slice off the top to make a lid. Scoop out the seeds with a teaspoon.

For the filling, heat oil in a pan and fry onion and garlic until softened. Stir in breadcrumbs, almonds and parsley and season. Mix thoroughly and carefully stuff each tomato cavity. Replace lids and place on a baking tray. Cook in a preheated oven at Gas 6 400F 200C for 5 minutes.

Little Savoury Eclairs

*Choux buns with cream cheese and
onion filling*

MAKES APPROX 24
Choux buns
1/4 pint/150ml milk and water mixed
2oz/50g butter
2 1/2 oz/65g plain flour
pinch of salt
2 eggs, beaten

Filling
8oz/225g cream cheese, softened
1 tbsp double cream
4 spring onions, finely chopped
salt and cayenne pepper

For choux, bring water and milk and butter to the boil. Add flour and salt and beat with a wooden spoon until mixture leaves the sides of the pan. Allow to cool slightly, then beat in eggs until glossy. Grease a baking tray and pipe 1"/2.5cm lengths, using a piping bag fitted with a 1/2"/1cm plain nozzle. Bake in a preheated oven at Gas 6 400F 200C for 10 minutes, then reduce heat to Gas 4 350F 180C and cook until golden and crisp.

For filling, beat cheese with cream, spring onions, salt and cayenne. Split each choux bun and pipe mixture along the centre. Top with lids to serve.

Quail's Eggs with Dipping Salts

*Hard boil the quail's eggs and serve them as they are
for guests to peel, or already shelled*

SERVES 12
2 dozen quail's eggs

Citrus salt
3 tbsp salt
finely grated zest of 1 lemon
finely grated zest of 1 orange

Chilli salt
3 tbsp salt
1 tsp chilli powder
1 tsp ground coriander
1/2 tsp turmeric

Pepper and fennel salt
3 tbsp salt
freshly ground black pepper
1 tsp fennel seeds, crushed
2 tsp ground bay leaves
2 tsp fresh thyme, chopped

Plunge quail's eggs into a pan of boiling water for 4 minutes. Lift out eggs and plunge into cold water. Remove shells immediately.

For citrus salt, mix ingredients together and spoon into a small pot. Repeat for chilli salt and for pepper and fennel salt.

Pile eggs into a bowl and dip into salts before eating.

Chicken Twizzles

*Thin strips of marinated chicken, twirled round a cocktail stick
or wooden skewer and grilled*

SERVES 10
4 chicken fillets, skinned

Marinade
6 tbsp olive oil
juice of 1 lemon
3 cloves garlic, crushed
2 tsp chilli powder
1 tsp ground coriander
1 tsp ground cumin
1 tbsp grated root ginger
salt

Flatten chicken fillets between two sheets of cling film or foil with a meat bat or rolling pin. Cut into thin strips. Secure one end of a chicken strip to a small wooden skewer. Wind the chicken around and secure the other end. Repeat with remaining chicken.

Mix marinade ingredients in a bowl. Lay chicken sticks in a shallow dish and pour over marinade. Leave for at least two hours.

Remove from marinade and grill until chicken is cooked through. Baste occasionally with marinade.

Garlic Mussels

*Mussels on the half shell topped with garlic,
parsley and Parmesan cheese*

SERVES 10
30 fresh mussels, washed and de-bearded
¼ pint/150ml dry white wine
1 bay leaf
sprig of parsley
4 cloves garlic, crushed
1oz/25g butter
2 tbsp finely chopped parsley
4 tbsp grated Parmesan
freshly ground black pepper

Discard any mussels that do not open when tapped with a knife, and any with cracked shells. Bring wine to the boil in a large pan, add herbs and mussels. Cover and steam mussels until shells open.
Strain and keep mussels hot. Remove any that have remained closed.

Carefully prise off the top shell of each mussel. Cook garlic in melted butter until softened. Stir in parsley and pile a little mixture on top of each mussel. Sprinkle with Parmesan and pepper and grill until cheese melts.

SOUL FOOD

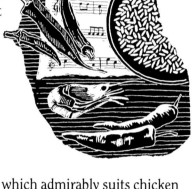

Country dishes from the deep south of America call for the accompaniment of Australian wines. Always the excuse for a family get-together, this distinctive and fragrant, down-to earth but nevertheless aesthetic food is a celebration in itself. The wines of Berri Estates partner it well.

One of the most famous Creole dishes is Jambalaya – the rice, chicken and seafood dish. Eat this with the Berri Estates Barossa Valley Sauvignon Blanc which admirably suits chicken and fish dishes – and particularly this one.

Gumbo is a hearty pork and okra stew with crab. A bottle of crisp, dry and peachy Renmano Chardonnay would be perfect with this – and with other pork and white meat dishes.

The nationally popular Southern Fried Chicken with its crisp spicy coating needs a Berri Estates Cabernet Shiraz. Smooth and spicy, this wine suits this dish well.

FOLLOWING PAGES, LEFT TO RIGHT:
*Southern Fried Chicken, Jambalaya,
Crab and Okra Gumbo*

Jambalaya

*Rice dish with prawns, chicken and ham cooked in stock
and spiked with a little chilli*

SERVES 4

4 tbsp oil
1 onion, peeled and finely chopped
2 cloves garlic, peeled and crushed
1 green pepper, de-seeded and cut into
  dice
8oz/225g long grain rice
1 tsp paprika
2 chicken breast fillets, skinned and cut
  into strips
2 thick slices smoked cooked ham, cut
  into chunks
1½ pt/850ml chicken stock
4oz/100g peeled prawns
2 tomatoes, peeled, de-seeded and cut
  into dice
good dash chilli sauce
salt and freshly ground black pepper

Heat 2 tbsp oil and fry onion, garlic and pepper until softened. Add rice and stir to coat. Stir in paprika and set aside.

In a separate pan heat remaining oil and cook chicken until browned. Add to rice mixture with ham. Pour on stock and bring to the boil. Simmer gently until rice is tender. Stir through prawns, tomato dice and chilli sauce. Season and pile onto a warmed serving platter.

Crab and Okra Gumbo

*Traditional gently spiced dish of pork, crab and okra
cooked in stock – a kind of thick soup served with rice*

SERVES 4

3 tbsp oil
1 lb/450g belly of pork
1oz/25g butter
1 onion, peeled and finely chopped
2 cloves garlic, crushed
2 sticks celery, trimmed and chopped
1 tbsp flour
1 tbsp tomato purée
1 tsp chilli powder
2 pints/1 litre vegetable stock
1 lb/450g okra, trimmed and washed
3 tomatoes, washed and chopped
8oz/225g crabmeat, flaked
dash Tabasco sauce
salt and freshly ground black pepper

Heat 1 tbsp of oil in a pan and brown pork on all sides. Remove with a slotted spoon. Add remaining oil and butter to pan and cook onion, garlic and celery until softened and golden. Stir in flour, tomato purée and chilli and cook for 1 minute. Return pork to pan and gradually pour on stock. Bring to the boil and simmer gently for 20 minutes. Stir in okra and tomatoes and continue cooking until tender. Stir through crab and season with Tabasco and salt and pepper. Serve straight from the pot with plain boiled rice.

Southern Fried Chicken

International favourite, originally from South America. Tender joints of chicken – buy the best – coated in spiced flour and deep fried in hot oil so the crust is crackly crisp and the chicken tender

SERVES 4

8 chicken joints
2 cloves garlic, crushed
2 tbsp oil
salt and freshly ground black pepper
3 tbsp flour, sifted
1 tbsp chilli powder
1/2 tsp cayenne pepper
good grating nutmeg
2 eggs, beaten
oil for frying
cherry tomatoes, halved, for decoration

Make slashes in the chicken with a sharp knife. Place in a bowl with garlic, oil and seasoning and toss to coat. Leave for 30 minutes.

Mix flour with spices and dip in chicken pieces. Shake off excess. Dip into egg and fry in hot oil until skin is crisp and golden and chicken is cooked through. Serve on a warm platter decorated with cherry tomatoes.

Red Beans and Rice

Simple but delicious mixture of spicy beans and rice

SERVES 4

2 tbsp oil
1 thick slice smoked bacon, cut into
  chunks
1 onion, peeled and finely chopped
2 large cloves garlic, crushed
2 sticks celery, trimmed and chopped
1/2 tsp cayenne pepper
1 tsp chilli powder
1 bay leaf
14oz/400g tin red kidney beans, drained
8oz/225g long grain rice
1 1/2pt/850ml vegetable stock
salt and freshly ground black pepper
good dash Worcestershire sauce and
  Tabasco

Heat oil in a pan and fry bacon until browned. Remove with a slotted spoon and reserve. Add onion, garlic and celery to pan and cook until softened. Return bacon to pan then stir in cayenne, chilli and bay leaf. Add beans and rice and stir well to mix. Pour over stock and bring to the boil. Simmer gently until rice is tender, adding a little more stock if necessary. Season with salt, pepper, Worcestershire sauce and Tabasco and pour into a warmed tureen to serve.

Creole Sweet Potatoes

*Delicious vegetable dish using sweet potatoes caramelised with a
little brown sugar, nutmeg and butter*

SERVES 4

*1½ lb/700g sweet potatoes, peeled and
    cut into thin slices
zest and juice of ½ lemon and ½ orange
3oz/75g butter
3 tbsp dark brown sugar
good grating of fresh nutmeg*

Bring a pan of lightly salted water to the
boil and add potatoes with lemon and
orange juice. Cook until just tender.
Drain.

Place in the base of a lightly buttered
ovenproof dish. Dot with butter and
sprinkle over sugar, zest and nutmeg.
Bake in a preheated oven at Gas 4 350F
180C for 20 minutes or until glazed and
syrupy. Cool slightly before serving.

81

Pecan Pie

*All-American pie in a shortcrust case with a filling of
halved pecans*

SERVES 6

*8oz/225g shortcrust pastry
3 eggs
8oz/225g brown sugar
8fl oz/225ml corn syrup
2oz/50g butter, melted
few drops vanilla essence
6oz/175g pecan nuts, halved
extra corn syrup for brushing*

Roll out pastry on a lightly floured board
to fit an 8"/20cm loose-bottomed flan
ring. Chill for 30 minutes.

Lightly beat eggs and sugar until thick
and frothy. Whisk in corn syrup and melted butter and vanilla. Arrange half the
nuts in the base of the pastry case and
pour over syrup mixture. Arrange
remaining nuts in a circular pattern on
top. Brush with corn syrup to glaze.

Place in a preheated oven at Gas 7 425F
220C for 10 minutes, then reduce tem-
perature to Gas 3 325F 160C for a further
35 minutes or until set. Serve with cream.

PENFOLDS

THE GRATE OUTDOORS

Scents, sights and savourings – all these attack the senses to make cooking and eating al fresco a most satisfying experience. From the moment the coals are lit, the first steaks and chops are on the grid, and the enticing aromas begin wafting towards nostrils, the scene is set for a gastronomic treat.

And the most appropriate wines to drink with a barbecue have to be Australian.

Find a wine in the Penfolds' range which includes exceptional red and white wines to match just about anything. Try marinated lamb steaks with herbs with a bottle of Bin 28 Kalimna Shiraz. Rich, full-bodied and smoothly fruity, this is the perfect complement. And with the home-made pepper steakburgers Penfolds' claret-style Koonunga Hill with its fresh berry fruit and soft finish is superb.

And no barbecue would be complete without copious supplies of something refreshingly sparkling – like the brilliant Seaview Sparkling wine, crisp, dry and satisfyingly biscuity with a brush of citrus acidity.

Grilled Sardines with Lime and Fennel

Sardines are cheap and tasty, and especially good
with lime and fennel

SERVES 4
12 sardines, gutted and washed
6 tbsp olive oil
juice and zest of 2 limes
1 clove garlic, crushed
3 tbsp fennel fronds, finely chopped
salt and freshly ground black pepper
fennel fronds and lime twists to decorate

Make small slashes on the sides of the sardines with a sharp knife. Mix oil, lime juice and zest, garlic, 2 tbsp fennel and salt and pepper in a bowl. Toss fish in this mixture and leave for 30 minutes.

Place fish on a hot barbecue and grill for 4 minutes each side or until cooked through. Arrange on plates and sprinkle with remaining chopped fennel. Decorate with lime twists and fennel fronds to serve.

Pepper Steakburgers

Tender steakburgers flavoured with garlic and onions
encased in a black pepper crust

SERVES 4
1½ lb/700g minced steak
3 cloves garlic, crushed
1 onion, peeled and finely grated
2 tbsp parsley, finely chopped
salt and freshly ground black pepper
3 tbsp black peppercorns
oil for brushing

Put steak in a large bowl and mix with garlic, onion, parsley and seasoning. On a lightly floured board, form into small burgers using hands. Crush peppercorns lightly by placing in a bag and tapping with a rolling pin. Dip burgers both sides into pepper to coat. Press in lightly.

Brush burgers with oil, place on a hot barbecue and cook for about 5 minutes each side or until cooked to preference. Serve in baps with salad.

FOLLOWING PAGES, ON THE BARBECUE, FROM TOP CLOCKWISE:
Marinated Lamb Leg Steaks, Vegetable Brochettes, Pepper Steakburgers, Grilled Sardines with Lime and Fennel

Marinated Lamb Leg Steaks

Meaty lamb steaks make the perfect barbecue feast. Soak them in a red wine marinade before grilling for extra juiciness

SERVES 4
4 large lamb leg steaks

For the marinade
½ pt/300ml red wine
4 tbsp oil
3 cloves garlic, peeled and halved
1 onion, peeled and sliced into rings
2 sprigs rosemary
1 bay leaf
few black peppercorns
salt and freshly ground black pepper

Wipe lamb and place in a shallow dish in one layer. Mix together wine, oil, garlic, onion, herbs and peppercorns. Pour over lamb, cover and leave for several hours, preferably overnight in the refrigerator.

Remove lamb from marinade and pat dry. Season with salt and pepper. Place on a hot barbecue and grill for about 6 minutes each side or until cooked on the outside and pink in the centre. Brush with a little marinade during cooking.

Vegetable Brochettes

These succulent skewers of vegetables are scented with lemon and aniseed and charcoal grilled

SERVES 4
2 courgettes, washed and cut into chunks
1 aubergine, washed and cut into chunks
8 cherry tomatoes
8 button mushrooms
4 bay leaves

For the baste
¼ pt/150ml oil
juice and zest of 1 lemon
2 tsp aniseeds, lightly crushed
salt and freshly ground black pepper

Thread vegetables onto skewers with bay leaves.

Whisk the baste ingredients together and brush over kebabs. Grill over charcoal, turning frequently until just tender.

Corn Cobbers

*Spicy butter is a perfect complement to
barbecued corn-on-the-cob*

SERVES 4
4 corn-on-the-cobs, husks removed

For the butter
4oz/100g butter
1/2 tsp mustard powder
1/2 tsp cayenne pepper
*garlic salt and freshly ground black
   pepper*

Blanch corn in lightly salted boiling water
for 5 minutes. Drain and place on the
barbecue for about 10 minutes to complete cooking, turning over occasionally.

Spike ends of corn with corn skewers and
arrange on a platter. Melt butter with
remaining ingredients in a small pan.
Drizzle over corn to serve.

Toffee Pineapple

*Fresh pineapple slices cooked wrapped in foil
with a tangy toffee syrup*

1 fresh pineapple
zest and juice of 1 orange
4oz/100g butter
4 tbsp dark brown sugar

Remove stalk from pineapple and cut into
four lengthways. Cut out the core from
each piece then slice thickly into triangles
without peeling.

Cut squares of foil and lay a few pineapple
slices on each one. Sprinkle with orange
zest and juice, dot with butter and
sprinkle with sugar. Wrap into parcels and
place on the barbecue. Cook until tender
and sauce is syrupy.

MITCHELTON

BIG DIPPERS

Rather an unusual way to entertain – the guests prepare and cook the meal themselves. A cheese fondue is inexpensive – and irresistible. This creamy and filling dip-and-twirl dish needs a fulsome dry white wine like Mitchelton's Wood Matured Marsanne with its oaky flavour and hints of honeysuckle and crisp lemon finish.
Try lamb, chicken or even fish fondues.
Same pot, same process, but for these fondues, the raw ingredients are cooked in a pot of oil for the lamb version, or in bubbling stock for the fish or chicken. The stock turns into flavourful soup to be eaten at the end of the meal.
The perfect Mitchelton wine to serve with a fish fondue is Thomas Mitchell Fumé Blanc – a bone-dry crisp and steely white wine with a soft fruity aroma. And with the lamb fondue, an Australian Cabernet Sauvignon like the excellent Mitchelton Goulburn Valley, a deep, vibrant red wine with a scent and taste of berry fruits.

Cheese Fondue

A cheese fondue party is the perfect way to entertain a crowd

SERVES 4
2 cloves garlic, peeled and halved
½ pt/300ml dry white wine
1 lb/450g Gruyère cheese
1 tbsp cornflour
2 tbsp Kirsch
freshly ground black pepper

Rub cut garlic surface around a fondue pot. Pour in wine and gently warm. Gradually add cheese in small pieces and stir vigorously until melted. Mix cornflour with Kirsch to a smooth paste and beat into cheese mixture. Continue to beat until smooth and thickened. Season. Serve with chunks of bread for dipping.

The fish broth, which is the basis of this fondue, gets tastier
with each piece of fish that is dipped in.
Serve surrounded with little pots of savoury sauces

SERVES 4
For the broth
1lb/450g white fish bones and trimmings
  (sole, whiting, cod)
1 onion, peeled and chopped
1 leek, white part only, washed and sliced
2 sticks celery, washed and chopped
1 fresh bouquet garni
few black peppercorns
2 pints/1 litre water
rosemary and parsley sprig and bay leaf
  for serving in broth

Selection of fish such as sole fillets,
rolled, Mediterranean prawns, red mullet
pieces, cooked mussels, and sprigs of
parsley for decoration

Fresh tomato dip
2 tbsp oil
2 shallots, peeled and finely chopped
1 clove garlic, crushed
1 tsp thyme, chopped
1 lb/450g tomatoes, peeled, de-seeded,
  and chopped
salt and freshly ground black pepper
pinch of sugar

Tartare sauce
4 tbsp ready made mayonnnaise
2 tbsp sour cream
4 small gherkins, chopped
1 tbsp capers, chopped
1 tbsp parsley, chopped
2 tbsp grated onion
salt and freshly ground black pepper

Béarnaise sauce
2 tbsp tarragon vinegar
2 tbsp white wine vinegar
1 shallot, peeled and finely chopped
2 egg yolks
4 oz/100g butter, melted
salt and ground white pepper
squeeze of lemon juice
1 tbsp chopped tarragon and parsley

Thoroughly wash fish bones and trimmings and chop up. Omit things like eyes and livers as this makes the broth bitter and cloudy. Place in a large pan with vegetables, herbs and peppercorns and pour over water. Bring to the boil and simmer for 20 minutes, skimming the surface occasionally. Strain and discard bones, vegetables and herbs. Reserve stock.

Arrange fish neatly on a serving platter and decorate with parsley sprigs. Chill until required.

For the tomato dip, heat oil in a pan and cook shallots and garlic until softened. Stir in thyme and tomatoes and cook until just beginning to pulp. Season and add sugar.

For the tartare sauce, mix mayonnaise and sour cream then add remaining ingredients. For the béarnaise sauce, place vinegars and shallot in a pan and bring to the boil. Reduce by half then cool and whisk in yolks. Place in a bowl over a pan of hot water and whisk until thickened and the mixture leaves a trail. Gradually whisk in butter. Season and add lemon juice, chopped tarragon and parsley.

Spoon sauces into pots. Reheat stock to boiling and pour into a fondue pot. Add fresh herbs.

To eat, dip each piece of fish to cook then into sauces to eat.

Lamb Fondue

*Tender nuggets of lamb spiked on a fondue fork and cooked in hot oil,
then dipped into mint or garlic dip*

SERVES 4

Mint dip
12 fresh sprigs of mint, leaves removed
    and finely chopped
1 tbsp white wine vinegar
½ onion, peeled and finely chopped
½ pint/300ml Greek yogurt
salt and freshly ground black pepper

Garlic dip
2 egg yolks
1 tsp mustard
6 cloves garlic, crushed
juice of ½ lemon
½ pint/300ml sunflower oil
salt and freshly ground black pepper

2 lb/900g leg of lamb, cubed and trimmed

For the mint dip, mix all ingredients and spoon into a serving pot.

To make garlic dip, put yolks in a bowl with mustard, garlic and lemon juice. Whisk in oil a little at a time until mixture thickens, then add remaining oil in a thin stream. Whisk until thickened, then season with salt and pepper.

Heat oil in a fondue. Arrange lamb on a serving platter and dip cubes with pronged forks into the oil until cooked to preference. Serve with dips.

Chocolate Fondue

*The ultimate indulgence for the chocoholic! Dip fruit,
sweet biscuits, marshmallows into this fantastic dreamy chocolate sauce*

SERVES 4
8 oz/225g milk chocolate
6 oz/175g plain chocolate
4 tbsp double cream
2 tbsp Grand Marnier

For dipping
A selection of fruit ie. banana chunks,
strawberries, cherries, grapes, apple
slices, orange segments

Crisp dessert biscuits, macaroons,
marshmallows, langues de chat, baby
meringues

To make the fondue, melt chocolate in a bowl over a pan of hot water. Stir in cream and Grand Marnier until smooth. Pour into a fondue pot over a low flame and surround with fruit and biscuits. Use skewers for dipping fruit and biscuits into chocolate.

Chicken Fondue

Delicious fondue where slivers of tender chicken are dipped into home-made chicken and vegetable stock, then into spicy tomato sauce

SERVES 4

For the stock

2 pints/1 litre home-made chicken stock, strained
1 onion, peeled and finely chopped
1 carrot, peeled and diced
1 leek, washed and sliced
2 tbsp fresh chives, snipped
salt and freshly ground black pepper

Spicy tomato sauce

1 tbsp oil
1 onion, peeled and finely chopped
1 clove garlic, crushed
1 chilli pepper, de-seeded and finely chopped
4 large tomatoes, peeled, de-seeded and chopped
good dash Worcestershire sauce and soy sauce
salt and ground black pepper

4 chicken breast fillets, skinned and cut into neat chunks

Pour stock into a pan and add vegetables and chives. Bring to the boil and pour into a fondue pot to keep hot.

For the sauce, heat oil and cook onion, garlic and chilli for 2 minutes. Add tomatoes, sauces, salt and pepper. Simmer until mushy. Spoon into a serving pot.

To serve, dip chicken chunks into hot stock on the end of skewers until cooked through. Dip into tomato sauce before eating. The stock is served as a soup afterwards.

Steamboat